Edward England, who inspired the *I Believe Series* published by Hodder and Stoughton, is the General Editor of this *We Believe Series* published by Marshall Morgan and Scott. The earlier series, edited by Canon Michael Green, was concerned with the theology of our faith. In each volume of this new series twelve or so contributors will make personal statements of faith, written from daily experience. The titles will include *We Believe in Marriage, We Believe in Mission, We Believe in Prayer* and *We Believe in Guidance*.

While Edward England is General Editor of the series each volume will have its own individual editor. *We Believe in Healing* has been prepared by his wife, Ann, who is an obstetrician and gynaecologist in Sussex.

We Believe in Healing

Edited by
Ann England

Marshalls

Marshalls Paperbacks
Marshall Morgan & Scott
1 Bath Street, London EC1V 9LB

ISBN 0 551 01014 2

Photoset by Rowland Phototypesetting Ltd
Bury St Edmunds, Suffolk
Printed in Great Britain by
Richard Clay (The Chaucer Press) Ltd,
Bungay, Suffolk

To the doctors who first helped
me to believe

Contents

Editor's preface

by Ann England

Doctors have always found it hard to believe that God heals miraculously. Our training gets in the way. We expect a disease to follow a particular course. But because of what we are observing today we are looking again at the healing miracles in the New Testament.

The woman with a high fever suddenly left her bed and waited on her guests; the paralysed man stood, picked up his bed and walked home. The blind man strode away from his begging place, his sight restored; a frantic demon-possessed man was found sitting quietly, clothed and rational. With power and authority Jesus rebuked disease and commanded evil spirits to leave their victims. People came to him in faith, 'Say the word and my servant will be healed.' A woman timidly touched the edge of his garment, believing. 'Your faith has healed you,' he said. 'Go in peace.'

The news about the Healer spread and great crowds came 'to hear him and to be healed of their diseases. Those troubled by evil spirits were cured, and the people all tried to touch him, because power was coming from him and healing them all' (Luke 6.18–19).

Jesus gave his disciples 'power and authority to drive out all demons and to cure diseases, and he sent them out to preach the kingdom of God and to heal the sick' (Luke 9.1–2). 'In the name of Jesus Christ of Nazareth, walk,' said the apostle Peter and the crippled man jumped to his feet and began to walk. 'Lord, stretch out your hand to heal,' prayed Peter and John and the sick were healed.

As a medical student I learned from experienced doctors by attending ward rounds, by listening and watching, but I saw nothing to match those open air 'clinics' which Jesus held. What a privilege to follow him on an emergency call to the convulsing boy or Jairus' dying daughter! Luke, the physician, wrote in his Gospel and in Acts accounts of many of the healings. As a doctor he was observant of detail: it was the man's right hand that was withered; the woman who had spent all her money on doctors had had a haemorrhage for twelve years; the crippled man who had been unable to walk from birth was forty years old.

I became a Christian while studying medicine in Cardiff. I was overwhelmed that God, formerly thought of as distant and uninvolved, actually knew and loved me. For as long as I could remember I had wanted to be a doctor. Now this determination had new meaning. My struggles to understand and memorise the intricacies of anatomy and physiology were lightened by an increasing inward delight at worshipping the God who had designed all this. I marvelled at his handiwork in the body's responses, the inbuilt mechanisms of defence against disease, of reaction and repair following medication or surgery.

In our clinical years we were taught to observe, examine and assess. The patient's symptoms and signs, once ascertained, could be fitted into a pattern, the cause determined, the outcome predicted. If sometimes it was difficult to fit an illness into a neat text book picture, we thought it would be easier when our knowledge and experience had increased.

Once qualified and taking responsibility for initial diagnosis and treatment it became more apparent that diseases are not so easily categorised. Patients had symptoms we had not learned about; responses varied. One recovered uneventfully, while another who had had a similar operation developed recurrent wound infections which prolonged the convalescence. A drug cured one, but had no effect on another with a seemingly identical disease. In time we began to understand a little more about the effect of the emotions and the importance of stress as a major contributor to illness. Stress is 'an inbalance between demand and the ability to cope which causes structural and functional damage if prolonged.' Even when the exact nature of stress can be determined there is little effective treatment. Medical knowledge is limited.

Most doctors recognise that a patient is more than a disease, that the soul and the spirit affect the body. They endeavour to care for the whole person, observing that a patient with faith and hope can withstand his illness better.

That a positive outlook is an important factor in assisting healing is increasingly recognised. An editorial recently in *The Lancet* on the theme 'Mind and Cancer' reported: 'There is a small body of research which suggests that certain emotional characteristics may be a factor in susceptibility to cancer, or may affect the prognosis from an existing cancer.' It noted that 'very powerful belief was a strong factor in the spontaneous regression of cancer seen in some patients.' As an adjunct to orthodox medical treatment some clinicians were training their patients to 'fight back' by picturing their tumours being overcome by the body defences. There was uncertainty whether the benefit claimed resulted mainly from hope, expectation and belief or other factors but 'it is almost certain that the absence of hope can shorten life, apart from vitiating its quality.'

Christian doctors believe that all healing is from God; that he can direct the surgeon's scalpel and the physician's therapy. They believe that God acts through natural mechanisms. Many consider that miracles of healing ended with the ministry of the apostles. That traditional view is one which I accepted when I went to Thailand as a missionary in 1963. I went in obedience to Christ's command to preach the gospel and to heal the sick. I prayed for my patients, I prayed for wisdom and skill, asking God to use my mind and my hands to bring healing. But I had little expectation of healing through other than medical means.

Yet, when a forty year old patient, a Christian, who had lost her first baby, was threatening to miscarry again, God gave me the faith to pray with her, thanking him for the healthy baby he was going to give her. Her distress and anxiety vanished, the pregnancy subsequently continued uneventfully and some months later I had the joy of delivering her son. I believed, and she believed, that as we prayed God had intervened.

Why as doctors are we so slow to believe? It goes back to our training. We learn facts and figures, basing treatment on statistical surveys and controlled clinical trials. If seventy-five per cent of patients with hypertension are cured by drug B and only ten per cent by drug A, then drug B becomes the standard treatment. The unexpected cure which every doctor sees, the unexplained response, is liable to be ignored as not statistically significant. Our years in medical school and in practice have taught us how the body functions in health and disease. We know what to expect and are inclined to question anything contrary.

When Christian doctors have considered faith healing they have often approached it similarly, requiring objective medical evidence of cured physical disease. There has been a tendency to dismiss healings of mental, emotional or psychosomatic illness however remarkable the improvement in the patient. Such healing does not show up on an X-ray. It is not subject to measurement. Therefore it is dismissed. Recently, however, *The Lancet*, in an article on stress in relation to disease, recommended, among other measures, that 'doctors should have greater knowledge of non-medical cures such as faith healing, since these cures may be more profound and enduring than those achieved by conventional medicine.'

Every doctor knows that while it is comparatively easy to treat abdominal pain due to appendicitis, it is almost impossible to cure 'psychosomatic' abdominal pain which persists and causes immense suffering in spite of extensive investigation and treatment. But God, I began to see, could not merely eliminate the symptoms but bring healing to the whole person. In fact, healing of the physical symptoms might be delayed as he began the cure at a deeper level. God knew the root of every problem, the hurts and scars of soul and spirit, as well as body.

With many others in the medical profession I had once doubted that anything could change the natural progression of a disease. I had been ready, indeed anxious, to dismiss what I could not explain. Then God, little by little, began to open my eyes through the ministry of the Holy Spirit in my own life. There was the occasion when I was on holiday with an American missionary. We sat over-looking the Gulf of Siam as she recalled a healing service which she had attended. Her account of a crippled woman getting up from her chair completely healed was so vivid that I felt as if I were there seeing fresh life entering those deformed limbs.

When I returned to England I discovered a whole new interest in the church's ministry of healing. I attended healing services. I listened to those who had been healed tell of what God had done. My doubts began to evaporate. I turned to the Bible but nowhere could I find any hint that healing miracles were limited to New Testament times. How could I have been so blind?

One of the special visitors we had to stay in our home was Canon Jim Glennon, who had held a weekly healing service in Sydney Cathedral for nearly twenty years. He ministered in our local church and stayed up late by our fireside answering questions. Before he left he gave me a report from a doctor in Australia who had endeavoured to pray individually for each baby and child while examining them. Two things had happened: the doctor found his patients were getting better faster than when other doctors treated them, and they had fewer complications. The medical care did not differ. This was far from the double blind trial that has come to be accepted in research but for me it had the ring of truth. I believed. The report concluded: 'It does seem reasonable to me that when we apply the principles of faith to our own work in this way and ask the Lord to heal, he will answer our prayer and that we may very well be astounded at the results.'

More and more Christian doctors, cautious by nature and training, are beginning to expect the unexpected. In ways that defy medical explanation they sometimes see instantaneous, sometimes gradual, reversals of the disease process. 'It's an answer to prayer,' they confess. 'God healed.' Some have received healing as I have.

In *We Believe in Healing* thirteen contributors, among them two other doctors, tell of their faith. They all face the ✳ fact that many are not healed. They have as many questions as answers. But all the writers accepted my invitation to contribute because they wanted to share in this prescription for faith.

As you read this book:
God may increase your faith.
God may heal you.
God may give you faith to pray for someone to be healed.
God may call you to a healing ministry.

✳ God's plan for our lives & growth in faith is a mystery to us — we only realise in retrospect.

The coming of Christ

Donald Bridge

The Rev. Donald Bridge is the minister of Frinton Free Church, Frinton-on-Sea, Essex. He is co-author with David Phypers of *Spiritual Gifts and the Church*, *The Water that Divides* and *The Meal that Unites?*

They say that our earliest memories are important, that if something stands out clearly from the hazy unformed recollection of very early childhood, there is a reason for it – and its influence is probably still with us.

In my case it seems to be so. My two earliest memories are closely related. A cloth-capped workman arrived at the door to say that my father was the victim of a serious accident in the factory. It nearly killed him, but he recovered. The same year I went down with measles and whooping-cough in quick succession. Forty-five years ago, amidst the poverty of the industrial north, both illnesses were afflictions to be dreaded. The long fever, the gummed-up eye-lids, the fear of being blind, the choking for breath, the long separation from playfriends – all this, with the shock of father's near death, left a legacy. For the next fourteen years bronchial asthma dogged my steps.

It is a strange affliction, understood nowadays to owe more to emotional than physical factors. It carried with it an outlook on life marked by timidity, depression, total absence of self-confidence, morbid introspection – and fear. Fear, most of all, of the long bleak nights (about one in four) when the heart raced, the chest contracted, the lungs fought for air.

In my teens, Christ found me. The faith transmitted in childhood by devout and loving parents was resisted for a time, and then became firmly and personally mine. The asthma did not disappear immediately, but an astonishing new sense of self-worth began to struggle through. Christ loved *me*!

One day a visiting preacher revealed an interest in an odd form of treatment called homeopathy. It made no sense, and I had long since lost any confidence in doctors (unfair but fact). But, perhaps for that very reason, I found a reluctant interest in someone who was not a doctor. We chatted. He seemed far more interested in me than in my symptoms. We bowed our heads and he prayed for me. After a quiet word with my parents, he left what looked for all the world like little packets of dog conditioning-powders.

I was not having an attack at the time, and the days stretched out without one. After a month, there was still no asthma. After two months it began to dawn on me that I was cured. It was as simple as that, and I have no explanation. At the age of sixteen, I climbed on to a bicycle for the first time. In the thirty-four years that have elapsed since, I have had one four-day attack, during a time of great emotional pressure.

My doctor, who watched all this, was impressed, irritated and dismissive all at the same time.

'Of course asthma doesn't have an organic or physical cause,' he explained to us. 'There's a word for it – psychosomatic. The effect of the mind, or soul, or inward being, upon the body. Quite common. In a way, the asthma never really existed. There was nothing to stop you breathing, Don. So this "cure" isn't a miracle or anything like that. Something in the fellow's attitude to you has given you confidence – it's *that*, not the sugar-and-whatnot in his little packets.'

I did not mean to be rude. I just wanted to know. I asked bluntly, 'Then if it's as easy as that, how come all your medicines haven't cured me in fourteen years?'

Of course the doctor was right in his explanation of asthma. Like a dozen other ailments, and a hundred other symptoms, it is psychosomatic. The word is a useful one. *Psyche* is the soul, or inward being. *Soma* is the body. Modern medicine has discovered what the Bible always maintained – that the two are inextricably bound together. Body and soul are not strictly separate entities, as the western world has often supposed. Nor is the body a mere prison for the soul, as the East is inclined to think. Hebrew thought, guided by the Old Testament, saw man as an entity in which the personality, the spiritual life and the body are all interdependent. The New Testament takes it for granted.

To modern medicine it is a fairly recent idea, but now accepted and indeed proved. Physical ailments really are often caused by inward attitudes, mental conditions and emotional shocks. Stomach ulcers are (sometimes) caused by worry. Arthritis seems to be (sometimes) linked with bitterness of spirit. Headaches can be caused by frustration, paralysis by guilt, asthma by fear. Depressed people are more open to infection. Anger releases a flow of harmful chemicals into the body. Hurt administered long ago poisons the subconscious memory and leads to illness.

Now notice something. I have mentioned worry, bitterness, frustration, guilt, depression, anger, and poisoned memory. These are all unchristian attitudes. The coming of Christ into a person's life confronts (to varying degrees) all of these attitudes with divine love and forgiveness and a new spirit. The psychosomatic becomes an area where the healing streams that flow from a saving God are specially at work.

My own experience is an example. What does it matter that the disappearance of asthma can be 'explained' as psychosomatic, as if that somehow makes it unnecessary to attribute it to God? The miracles of Christ were not specially designed to make scientists gasp or to deny the laws of nature. They were signs of God's grace, signs of the impact of his Kingdom, signs of the compassion of Jesus.

That is what came to me – and I have seen it touch very many others.

There are three ingredients in everyday church life which bear powerfully upon these areas. We have Christ's answer to guilt, the Christian experience of peace, and the church's life of community.

Guilt – and Christ's gift of forgiveness

'Your sins are forgiven,' declared Jesus. Sometimes physical healing followed forgiveness (Mark 2.1–12). Sometimes emotional peace went with it (Luke 8.42–48). This is the fundamental purpose of the Gospel – and its most thrilling and liberating feature. 'Whenever the church proclaims the forgiveness of sins, there the healing ministry is veritably at work,' says James Stewart.

To be able to sing . . .

> 'My sin, oh the bliss of this glorious thought,
> My sin, not in part but the whole,
> Is nailed to His cross and I bear it no more,
> Blessed hope, blessed rest of my soul!'

. . . is to release tides of inner healing. In modern life there seems at first to be little awareness of sin because God is forgotten. In fact, all that has happened is that the *guilt* (which every doctor and psychiatrist knows perfectly well is there) has been driven deeper and become disguised because modern godless man no longer understands why he feels it.

'The bad conscience,' writes Emil Brunner, 'is like a dog which is shut up in the cellar on account of its tiresome habit of barking. It is continually on the watch to break into the house which is barred against him, and is able to

21

do so the moment the master's vigilance is relaxed. The bad conscience is always there, it is chronic.'

True. And the airy assurance of humanistic psychiatrists, permissive counsellors and trendy clerics that sin doesn't matter, does not silence the accusing voice. It only makes guilty people feel that they are foolish and guilty for feeling guilty.

The forgiveness of God through the sin-bearing Saviour has three components. People aware of the first, often fail to realise the healing and liberating potential of the other two.

(a) *God forgives me*

Simple, vibrant statement! 'Who is a God like unto thee, that pardoneth iniquity, passeth by transgression, and delighteth in mercy' (Micah 7.18). He does so by providing One who was 'bruised' for those iniquities and 'wounded' for those transgressions (Isaiah 53.5).

(b) *I forgive myself*

That should certainly follow. How can I be more particular than God? How can I say, 'God has forgiven me and accepted me, but I will not forgive myself and I cannot accept myself'? But many do say this, including some who are impeccable in their orthodox evangelical faith. The assurance of God's forgiveness remains outside there, somewhere. It has not become subjective, felt, experienced in the realm of deep inner peace.

The result is the perfectionist. He is demanding and impatient. She is dutiful and she nags those who are not. They drive others *because they are being driven themselves*.

Another result can be the emotional cripple – timid, needing reassurance, desperate to have it proved repeatedly that he is loved, deeply hurt if criticised.

Both can reap a crop of physical symptoms, too – migraine, asthma, tension-pains, sleeplessness, high blood-pressure, indigestion, ulcers.

Protestants have their doubts about the Catholic practice of Confession. That is understandable. But a kind of non-compulsory evangelical confessional is often badly needed in the most Protestant of companies. Every pastor and counsellor knows it perfectly well. Quiet acts of penitence and assurances of pardon, meditative readings from the Scripture, sometimes the laying-on of hands – these are ways in which self-acceptance comes to the injured person who has found but not yet felt the forgiveness of God.

(c) *I forgive others*
And there's the rub! I really must. I have no option. The Bible links God's forgiveness of me with my forgiveness of others. (Matthew 18.35, Luke 11.4). So close is the link that some Christians feel that it threatens the freeness of God's grace. It does not, of course. God does not say, 'My forgiveness to you is a reward for your forgiveness to someone else.' God is the initiator, not the imitator. What he says is – 'A man who refuses to forgive someone else a minor injury thereby shows that he has not grasped the fullness of my forgiveness to him of the most colossal injuries.' (See the parable of the Two Debtors, Matthew 18.23–35.)

It can work both ways. A fresh touch from God can illumine in my soul a new awareness of the fullness of his forgiveness. The result is a surge of forgiving attitudes to others. Or the other way round. Determination to forgive someone else leads to a cry to God for grace to do so. The cry is answered – and in the answer comes a new awareness of his pardoning love.

One way or the other, it must happen. That cold, hard stone of resentment, hatred or injury plays havoc. It is an inner poison – a running sore in the spirit, in the memory, in the very body itself. It can cause everything from stomach ulcers to depression. I have counselled Christians sick in body or mind because of inability to forgive the long-ago beating by a parent, the immorality of a father, sexual interference from an uncle, humiliation from a school-teacher, betrayal of a friend, unfaithfulness of a lover, mockery of a fellow-student, or injustice of an employer. Sometimes it is clear on the surface. Sometimes it is half-hidden – a date on the calendar, a time on the clock, a remembered scent or a familiar view bringing it back in disguise.

Sometimes it will melt away as the Gospel is preached. I recall Sybil, who slipped into our services but claimed to be an unbeliever. We knew that life had treated her cruelly and that depression and despair and asthma crippled her. Offered friendship and prayer, she shrugged. 'The prayer won't work. There's no one there to listen.' One evening, hearing the story of the Cross retold, she melted in tears – and remained to take Communion. 'I felt the load lifting!' she exclaimed afterwards. The truth came out then. She had been a practising Christian years ago, led to Christ and baptised by a world-famous preacher. An act of disobedience and folly had put her at the mercy of a thoroughly bad man, and years of successive disasters had followed. She could not forgive the man, and she could not forgive herself. Nor could she forgive God. But then the old story of his forgiveness came with renewing power, and all was made new.

Sometimes it has to be wrestled with and cast out. The very memory of the unpardoned and unpardoning incident has to be recalled, submitted to the dismissing power of the Living Christ, and then forgotten. 'Picture it in your mind as it happened,' I have quietly advised. 'Replay the incident before your imagination while we pray in silence together. When it happened you did not know Jesus. Now you do. He is the same yesterday, today and forever, so invite him *now* into what happened *then*. Imagine him walking into that room and washing it all away.' They do . . . and he does.

24

Fear – and the Spirit's gift of peace

If guilt is the commonest cause of psychosomatic illness, fear comes a close second. 'Phobia' it is called in scientific jargon. 'Irrational fears' is a frequent term. These fears seem irrational because the cause appears to make no sense, and because simple logical reasoning has no effect on them. A curious example was the lady in the Nevada desert who became terrified of being attacked by sharks, after watching the film Jaws! The fact that there was no water within miles meant nothing – fear of sharks kept her indoors. What had happened, of course, was that the film had provided a vehicle and a disguise for a quite different fear deep within her.

Peace in place of fear is a very special gift of Christ, ministered by the Holy Spirit. 'Let not your hearts be troubled . . . believe in me . . . Peace I leave with you; my peace I give to you . . . Let not your hearts be troubled, neither let them be afraid' said Jesus (John 14.1 and 27). He still speaks those words, and applies them, when believing and expectant prayer shares them with the troubled sufferer. The root of the matter may still have to be searched for, and dealt with when it is understood, but both the revealing and the healing are the Spirit's work. 2 Timothy 1.6–7 links together the gifts of the Spirit, the laying-on of hands, and the dismissing of the spirit of fear.

A pathetic example was an elderly lady whom I visited in a Christian 'Home for the Aged'. She suffered from the most irrational fears, which in turn led to irrational behaviour. The hair on my head prickled as I sat in her little room on a dark autumn afternoon and listened to her.

'I'm the Great Harlot from the Book of Revelation,' she explained nervously. 'I don't want to be, but I cannot help it. I think the most horrible and lustful thoughts about the kings and rulers of the world. They come to my bed in the night and we do terrible things. I'm the Scarlet Woman and I will burn forever.'

It was a sick and confused shadow of some of the symbolic language of the Apocalypse. Gentle questioning elicited the fact that when she was a child her father had regularly chosen chapters from Revelation to read aloud to her in bed. There had been no explanation and no comment. She was a Christian but she still had not the remotest idea of the symbolic nature of that book.

In this case the healing came so quickly and easily that one could only groan – '*Why* did someone not do it years ago?' I explained to her the way to understand apocalyptic writing. I read the words of peace just referred to. There was not even the laying-on of hands. In a deep silence we could hear the final chirruping of birds as the autumn dusk fell over the garden outside. It was done. When her holiday was over she wrote from home a letter that was lucid, calm, joyful. The dark shadow had fled.

Tom's life had a shadow over it, too. He had watched his little child die and the horror of it had clutched his heart and mind ever since. Christian love at that time had brought him to real commitment, but the horror clung. He feared 'starting another family'. Mental depression created physical exhaustion in his work. He was the victim of obsessive and shameful thoughts about other people, their families, their sex life. Two long sessions of counselling enabled him to understand more clearly what was happening. The laying-on of hands and the invitation of Jesus *now* to go back into Tom's *then* . . . and peace flooded in, bringing an end to the physical exhaustion and the mental obsessions.

Loneliness – and the church's community life

'You seem to be a reconciled and forgiven people.' They were lovely words, and they were said by a rather way-out young couple who asked for an interview with me after attending my church for several weeks.

The story tumbled out: a typical tale of the brokenness, loneliness and bitterness that vaunted permissiveness brings in its wake.

I often remember them, for they sum up so well what others ought to be able to discern in any congregation of Christians. If we truly 'welcome one another as Christ has welcomed us' (Romans 15.7) we have, quite unconsciously, a powerful weapon of healing in our hands. A people for God who are learning to forgive each other, welcome each other, help each other and live with each other will carry, almost without noticing it, hope for the hopeless, reconciliation for the alienated and friendship for the lonely. Tragically, many of our churches have utterly failed here. The way we sit well apart from each other (usually at the back, to avoid the preacher!) – the way we keep greetings to a civil minimum – the way we define reverence as long face and dark clothes – the way we look furtively at a stranger who (astonishingly) attends – the way we insist on music and words meaningful only to the traditional in-group – these, and a dozen others, are warning signs which flash out the message *keep away*, even while we paste up outside a poster which proclaims, *Christ receiveth sinful men*.

And outside are the broken, the lonely, the heart-sick, the rejected. They look for some shallow touch of community in the pub, the coffee bar, the disco, the bingo hall.

Trevor was such a person. Aged eighteen when I first met him, he was morose, round-shouldered, untidy, greasy-haired. His feet scraped the ground as he walked, and a stammer destroyed his few efforts to converse. He suffered from epilepsy which was not always held in control by medication. At a fairly early date shamed parents had rejected him in quite specific terms as useless and hopeless. Schoolchildren, with that horrifying cruelty of which they are capable, made a splendid discovery. If they walked slowly towards him pointing their fingers at his face, he went into convulsions. They did – often.

Leaving school, he managed to hold down a job as a grave-digger. Somehow he wandered into our church. Silent, gloomy, with a chip on his shoulder that was almost visible, he attracted quiet pity and gentle friendship. Some of our polytechnic students 'adopted' him. Companionship, public worship, the preaching of the Word, youth outings, all began to have their effect. Still silent or stammering, he began to square his shoulders and sometimes to smile.

After three months I was giving him a lift in my car when the chance arose to press him ever so slightly about his faith. He said that he wanted to believe – perhaps *did* believe. Bible-reading had become a habit, fumbling attempts to pray were gaining confidence.

'How about Jesus Christ?' I asked, as I braked and he prepared to climb out.

He blinked up at me through his thick spectacles. 'Well . . . I believe that he died for me on the cross, and I've thanked him' (no stammering). He lifted his chin and looked straight in my eyes for the first time.

'Mr Bridge, he's forgiven me. I believe that. And accepted me.'

I drew a deep breath. 'Trevor, would you be willing to stand up in church on Sunday and say so?' He agreed immediately.

I wondered whether I had been wise. The church was crowded for a guest-service. When I announced Trevor's name several people gasped and others looked at the ground in embarrassment. One deacon whispered to his wife, 'Whatever is Don up to? The lad can't even *talk*!'

Trevor squared his shoulders and looked steadily over the congregation. The silence could be felt. Without a tremor he spelled it out: his discovery of a Saviour, his certainty of forgiveness, his place of acceptance in the fellowship. Some were quietly weeping as he walked back to his pew.

At my 'Wednesday Surgery' that week a charming and sophisticated lady booked in to consult me. As she sat down opposite me, she suddenly began to cry, the tears playing havoc with her eye-shadow and face-powder.

'That lad Trevor,' she murmured shakily, when she had recovered a little, 'I know him well. The difference in him on Sunday was incomprehensible. If God can do that for him, then I want to be a Christian.'

Two months later – 'You'd better go to the Baptist Church – the sooner the better,' said the Council foreman to Ted, another morose misfit. 'See what they've done for Trevor.' So Ted came, and his epilepsy went, too. Freda followed him with the same problems, and found the same answer.

It happens constantly

Our world is full of people like Sybil, like my elderly friend, like the way-out young couple, like Trevor and Ted and Freda. The church has the message that can bring them to God, and in its corporate life the community that can nurture them and bring them to greater wholeness. That, in my book, is healing. One form of healing, at any rate. There are others, of course. But I very specially believe in this. I have given examples from years ago in a different town. But similar things happen all the time. If they do not happen weekly, I am disappointed; if they did not happen monthly, I would be worried. For Christ came that we might have life, and have it more abundantly.

Either way – I win

Noreen Riols

Noreen Riols, A Christian writer and broadcaster now resident in France, tells of her husband's sudden heart attack and the bid to save his life.

'Do you mean there's no hope?' I stammered unbelievingly.

It was my husband's life I was talking about.

The surgeon didn't answer immediately, just looked at me kindly and as the white walls of the hospital corridor seemed to close in and suffocate me I waited for his reply. After an eternity it came.

'There is always hope,' he said quietly, and turned away.

And in that moment it seemed as if my life also turned away, away from all the happy, comfortable things I had known and taken for granted during more than twenty years of marriage, away from the cosiness of my daily routine, my family, my security.

I had been waiting outside the door of the intensive care unit behind which they were fighting for my husband's life, and, as the nurses passed noiselessly to and fro, I faced the fact, the terrible realisation, that before the day was over I might be a widow. Inside me was a dreadful void, an aching emptiness; death was something which broke into the lives of other people but not into ours. And in the antiseptic stillness I clung desperately to the fact that there is always hope.

Jacques had never been ill, not really ill, until that cold January morning two weeks earlier when my bed-making had been interrupted by a telephone call telling me that he had had a heart attack and been taken to a Paris hospital.

From that moment everything became unreal. As the days passed, he slowly weakened. Then yesterday, a Friday I was never going to forget, one of the best known cardiac surgeons in France had performed a difficult and, in 1975, relatively, unknown, heart operation in a bid to save his life.

As they wheeled Jacques from his room to the Operating Theatre I walked beside the trolley, holding his hand. He had been so confident, so full of hope that even when the nurse handed me his glasses and his wedding ring and the door leading to the theatre closed behind them, leaving me standing alone in that sterile corridor, some of my husband's peace remained. I felt that underneath me were the everlasting arms of Jesus carrying me over the angry waves which had threatened to engulf me during the past two weeks.

And yet, twenty-four hours later, the surgeon's unspoken words told me that he had done his best and now all we could do was hope.

The walls of the hospital revolved around me as I was helped into a gown and mask and allowed to see my husband. But that still figure on the bed, hung about with bottles and complicated apparatus, was not the smiling, confident man whose hand I had held the day before. Jacques no longer looked human, yet alone alive, though when he saw me standing beside him he tried to smile. The effort was too much: waves of pain and fatigue showed in his grey face and the nurse took my arm and led me away.

In a daze I stumbled down the interminable white corridors and out of the hospital into the pale afternoon sunshine. It was a beautiful, gentle day such as we often have in France in early February. The air was like champagne, soft and scintillating, but I was unaware of the world around me. All I could see was blinding, sterile whiteness and that grey, lifeless figure on the bed. Reaching the car park I wrenched open the door and crumpled against the steering wheel, sobbing helplessly.

Jacques was fifty-three. The youngest of our five children was not yet ten years old. How could God do this to us? How could he even think of taking him away when we needed him so much? And, as a blind fury surged up inside me against this loving Father who, I felt, had cheated us so badly, I drove miserably home, tears of anger and self-pity streaming down my face.

When I arrived the sun had gone, the short winter day was over and darkness had fallen; the children were all away and the house looked like an empty shell. As I put my key in the lock the window panes, cold and uninviting against the undrawn curtains, reflected my desolation and loneliness. It was Saturday evening, usually a warm, happy, family time with tantalising smells wafting from the kitchen, a log fire crackling in the hearth and the children and their friends coming noisily in and out. But today, as I stepped into the hall, the emptiness of our home echoed the bleak desolation in my heart and I wondered if anything would ever be the same again.

The long evening hours stretched ahead of me, and I didn't know what to do with them. There was no point in going back to the hospital, yet the tension and the unanswered question inside me hammered at my brain. I picked up the telephone.

A sympathetic voice answered my call.

'You must be worn out,' said the nurse who had led me from my husband's side. 'Why don't you go to bed and try to get some sleep? I promise we'll ring if there is any change – either way.'

As I put down the receiver an icy band of fear enclosed and squeezed my heart; that 'either way', had struck a chord of dread and finality. There were only two ways – either Jacques would recover . . . or he would not. And I did not want to face the second eventuality.

I sat down in the cold sitting room by the dead ashes in the grate, hardly noticing the rising moon shining in through the undrawn curtains. Everything was the same

. . . and yet nothing was the same. One person had been stricken and the whole household had fallen to pieces.

As I sat there, numb with cold and fear, from somewhere deep in my subconscious words I had once read came to my mind and I remembered the prayer of relinquishment. I had never given it a second thought because I had never needed it but now I clutched at this one straw, this chance to hand over the burden and the agony and just rest in Jesus.

Without realising what I was doing, I dropped to my knees, my head resting against the chintz-covered arm of the chair.

'Oh Father,' I breathed, 'you know how lonely and lost I feel. You know how much Jacques means to the children and me and how we need him, but you know, too, what is best for him. So tonight I thank you for the years we've had together, but if the time has come for him to go home I give him back to you wholeheartedly.'

I paused, the full realisation of what I had said suddenly hitting me, but I felt no fear. I lifted my head. The round yellow moon flooded the darkened room with a pale light, and I could see the smiling photograph of Jacques and the children taken in the garden only a few months before.

And for the first time that day, I smiled too.

'I'm going to bed now Father,' I went on, 'and I'm going to sleep because in your Word you promised to give your beloved sleep and tonight I feel I am your beloved. Thank you for that assurance and thank you for your love and care even when we don't always see your wisdom in what is happening in our lives. I won't telephone the hospital until the morning and then, whatever the answer, I will accept it, knowing that it's your plan for Jacques' life.'

I got up from my knees, drained and at peace.

The bells from the old church at the top of the hill were

ringing for Matins when I awoke next morning, refreshed after almost ten hours dreamless sleep.

Calmly I lifted the telephone, dialled the hospital number and asked for news.

'Your husband has had a good night,' came the reply.

I felt nothing but that immense peace.

For another forty-eight hours Jacques' life still hung in the balance then, slowly, his heart gained strength. But the incision on his chest refused to heal. A month later they operated again, yet when the stitches were removed the flesh parted and the great, gaping wound was revealed.

In early May a third operation was performed, but to no avail, and after four months in hospital one lovely late Spring afternoon Jacques was sent home, a sick man with a messy wound which had to be dressed twice a day.

The children were overjoyed to have him back and the two youngest spent the morning tearing up old sheets, making them into banners and streamers on which they had painted 'Welcome Home Daddy' before hanging them from every window. But the daddy who came home was not the daddy who had played football and swum with them a few months earlier. He was a weak man who walked like a monkey, arms dangling forwards, because of the wound and the constant pain in his chest. The children soon learned that life was not going to be as before and mentally backed away.

The hospital was unable to help us further and suggested we consult a chest surgeon and allergy specialist. We even tried a homeopath and our local G.P., but nothing worked. And when, a year later, a fourth operation was suggested in an attempt to close the gaping wound Jacques was so weak that he declined and we decided to hand over entirely to the Lord.

Our Christian friends were a great comfort to us during this time and one evening we had a laying-on of hands service for Jacques in our home when we read James' Epistle and claimed the promise of healing. At the end

Jacques, whose deep, quiet faith, unlike mine, had never wavered or doubted during all these trails, smiled up at me and said: 'Either the Lord takes the sickness from me, or me from the sickness – either way, I win.'

And having placed himself entirely in his Saviour's hands, at peace, he awaited his Lord's decision.

It did not come immediately.

Another year of pain and weakness went by. Somehow, we just lived from day to day, Jacques, serene and hopeful, I often down. In the end, it was he, the sick man, who was holding me up and carrying me through.

Then one Sunday in the Spring of 1977, over two years after the first operation, we went to Paris to an evangelistic service in a church at which we occasionally worshipped. At the end of the service the pastor said: 'I feel there is someone here who is in need of healing. Let us praise the Lord and pray for him or her.'

He must have been very sensitive to the Holy Spirit's leading that evening because it was not his custom to do this and I don't think he had ever done it before. Jacques and I were surprised and both wondered who that person could be.

My husband was very quiet on the way home, but when we arrived he said: 'Something very strange happened to me during that healing prayer. I suddenly began to shake uncontrollably and felt as if an electric current were going through my chest.'

I looked at him in amazement. Jacques is not what everyone imagines a typical Frenchman to be; he is, in fact, quite the reverse, quiet, reserved, unemotional. I am the 'up and down' one in our partnership. Quickly I began to undo his bandages, but the wound looked exactly the same.

My 'down syndrome' went into immediate action.

But the next morning Jacques got up earlier than usual and, after a few minutes, came back into the bedroom wearing only his pyjama trousers.

'Look,' he said quietly.

It was Monday. Spring seemed to have stopped suddenly and rain was spattering against the window panes. The alarm wasn't due to sound for another fifteen minutes and all I wanted to do was remain unconscious and not face the day. But he shook me gently and, unwillingly, I opened one eye then, abruptly, sat up.

Jacques was standing by the bed smiling his gentle, confident smile, but it wasn't his smile which hypnotised me, it was the long, clean, pink scar on his chest.

For a moment we neither of us spoke, then the full implication of what had happened hit me. Jesus had touched his sick body and made him whole, just as the Bible had promised he would. I had read about Jesus' power to heal so many times and heard it preached from the pulpit but even though I was a Christian it had seemed remote and not for today: beautiful miracles which happened two thousand years ago. But now I realised that miracles were for today after all, and were not only events which happened when Christ walked the earth as a man. They were happening, had happened here, in our own family. And I remembered Jesus' words: 'When the Holy Spirit comes upon you, you will do even greater miracles than I.'

And I was shattered at our lack of faith.

Why are we so reluctant to believe in the power of our living Lord working in and through our lives? Twelve hours earlier someone had stepped out in faith, sensitive to the Holy Spirit's prompting, and claimed healing for an unknown person in his congregation and Christ's power had poured through him.

I got out of bed feeling very humble but very grateful for the faith of those who believed strongly enough and dared to claim this power which can be ours if we belong to Jesus.

That was over five years ago.

Within three weeks of his healing this man who had not

had the strength to walk from the station to our house, who had been unable to turn over in bed without pain in his chest or put on his coat unaided, the man for whom the doctors could do no more, was digging the garden, kicking a football with his sons and running in the woods with the dogs.

And now, at sixty, he is stronger and busier than he ever was before that fateful January morning in 1975.

When the Lord heals he doesn't do it by halves.

Is it a coincidence that the scar on his chest now looks like a cross?

Healing in the local church

Bert Jordan

The Rev. Bert Jordan, of the United Reformed Church, lives in Birmingham and is the author of *On Roads to the Healing Christ*. He has seen many healings which cannot be explained in human terms. His long pastoral ministry has included healing missions and part time chaplaincies in psychiatric and general hospitals.

I was invited to conduct a healing service in a Midlands church in the spring of 1979: it was to be a quiet act of worship and teaching to introduce a healing ministry. That service proved to be the beginning of healing for one woman who, for the previous eight months, had been having injections for leukaemia. She writes to me: 'One of the side effects of the injections was a feeling whenever I swallowed anything that I was drinking a too-hot liquid. I was very keen to attend the service although I had moved some miles from the church and was far from well.'

It was a young layman who laid hands on her in prayer during the service and I was able to talk with her and her husband before they left for home. She speaks of the feeling of peace during the service and says that the 'swallowing' symptoms cleared quickly and did not recur although she continued regular injections for four months.

'I was,' she says, 'and still am, under the care of a very kind and concerned haematologist, but have had no treatment now for two and a half years. He told me after two years without treatment a recurrence is unlikely. I am now able to lead a normal and active life.'

In her letter this lady expresses a very confident belief that the prayers of many people have been of enormous value in her recovery from acute myeloid leukaemia, and that such prayers have backed up the treatment given by her doctor and the help of a loving and caring family. It seems that the Christian Church today is taking more seriously the command of its Lord to couple the preaching of the gospel with the healing of the sick. I have no doubt that in this sphere, as in many others, God is prompting his people to a deeper awareness of the power released by prayer. Jesus prayed and apparently felt the need of it. What fools we are to carelessly – or arrogantly – act as if we can manage without it. If mountains are to be removed, the Church must pray!

However, whatever emphasis you may put on the need for faith or compassion or prayer or any other human contribution, the underlying truth is that healing is God's response to human need: the response of that loving and healing Father seen so clearly in the life and ministry of Jesus. It is the continuing work of the risen Lord who has promised to be with us. This puts prayer in its proper place! Not a presumptuous demanding that God will make his ideas fit in with ours, not an unmanly grovelling as if we were asking a favour of a reluctant father, but the pipeline through which God can channel his power. The Christian faith offers a partnership, exemplified in the story of the man healed by the temple gateway (Acts 3). Peter and John admitted that they had nothing to offer (not even the odd coin to flip into the beggar's bowl). What they *could* do was to link the man's need with divine resources. And they did! Peter stretched out his hand to lift the man to his feet – a most unhelpful thing to do unless a man is pretty sure of his risen Lord. Of course there are problems. Of course there are questions about healing that cry out for an answer. And there should be a reason for the faith that is in us. But there are some certainties that cannot be denied though they can never be 'proved'. It does not make good scientific sense to argue that what goes beyond the present limits of human understanding is therefore impossible. It would be like telling the Creator that he cannot do anything unless the human mind can understand what he is doing. Scores of men and women have known healing that cannot be explained in human terms yet cannot be denied in experience. Perhaps we put too much emphasis on our problems and too little on our certainties. Remember the blind man whom Jesus healed? He was questioned pretty roughly by unbelieving Pharisees and didn't appear to know very much. He said he didn't know who Jesus was, or where he was or how he had restored his sight. One thing he did know. Once he was blind but now he could see! Splendid experiences come to us in quiet trust and faith but we are afraid of being credulous and we nurture the doubts that neutralise our glad certainties. It is foolish to live in poverty when we might be rich and to remain blind when we are offered clear vision. Moreover, the gospel is much clearer about the command to preach and heal than we are ready to admit.

It was the prompting of God's Spirit that led me into a ministry of prayer and healing – a ministry that has enriched my pastoral caring beyond measure. I hesitated before entering upon it, fearing failure. I wanted everything explained, and insisted that I needed proof, but in my best moments God seemed to be saying to me, 'Why *must* you know all the answers? I'm not asking you to do anything alone. Indeed, in this ministry you can't do anything without my help!' I needed to realise my own helplessness and the sheer inadequacy of my own efforts before I could take a step of faith which led to the point where God could use my obedience.

I had been in the full-time ministry for some seven or eight years and must confess that the healing ministry never had much of a place in my thinking. It certainly had not been part of my training. Pastoral work had become more of a burden than a joy and I would reach home at the end of the day with a deep and disturbing feeling of utter failure. True, I had dutifully visited the sick and fulfilled those regular pastoral tasks which should have brought some satisfaction, but at night, as I gathered the needs of

44

my people in prayer, the heartbreak came. I had left some in pain, or sleepless or full of anxiety or fear, yet the gospel cried aloud that the Lord whose servant I was could do so much more if I would take him at his word. Indeed he can! The simple truth, now demonstrated in the experience of many years, is that in the quiet act of prayer, as hands are lovingly laid upon those who are ill, pain can often be eased or banished, sleep can be induced and natural healing accelerated. And this, of course, is but part of the gracious ministry of wholeness our Lord wants for us. Hurtful memories can be healed, resentments lifted from the deep places where they fester and do so much harm, situations may be changed in ways that seem little short of the miraculous. It is a wonderful experience to see the evidence of Christ's healing and renewing power as we wait with a trustful humility upon him.

In my book *On Roads To The Healing Christ*[1] I have examined the events on some New Testament roads and linked those happenings with the experiences of my own ministry on the roads of every day. Each story is authenticated by those involved and tells of the healing Lord to be met on every road when we are sensitive to his presence.

I have permission to share with you the story of healing which came to the wife of a young colleague in the United Reformed Church ministry. The spinal trouble from which she suffered caused severe and constant pain over a period of some eleven or twelve years. In spite of much care, prolonged hospital treatment, and every kind of therapy, her condition and the pain got worse. Her husband came with her to my home where my wife and I received them and we had a cup of tea together. It was all deliberately informal. We came quietly to prayer as I laid my hands upon her head and then upon her back. It was simply and quietly done and within a few minutes she was

[1] Bert Jordan, On Roads to the Healing Christ (Arthur James Evesham).

able to stand and move and even touch her toes. There was no pain or discomfort. For the following twelve hours or so the feeling of warmth which so often comes with a healing ministry continued and a tingling sensation gave her the impression that 'things were being put right'. There was no pain or discomfort during the ministry – and none since. She gave testimoney to her healing at a conference some eighteen months after her experience and confirms it as I write – now nearly three years since her healing.

Such healing is not confined to the physical (though to be freed from pain, to be able to move freely and with no need for further regular and painful therapy is a blessing for which to thank God). I would never belittle the value of healing that appears to be merely physical, but the church's healing ministry offers much more than that. There is often a deep underlying healing that affects home and family and relationships. In the case of my colleague, the church was widened and enriched as the healing ministry took on a new significance among his people. This is a ministry of wholeness, of changed and renewed lives, of awakened awareness of the promises of Jesus to be with us.

Few would argue with the truth that Jesus sent his disciples out to preach the good news of the kingdom and to heal the sick. This happened in New Testament days and most are prepared to accept it. But when you look at the needs of men and women in this age, it makes nonsense of the gospel to suggest that healing was exclusively for the use of the early days of the Christian Church. Today's need is obvious. Over-worked doctors and social workers know the frustration of having little time to deal with the demands made upon them. And however willing they may be to give of their time, those who try to be helpful are confronted with much need – sometimes desperate need – that is beyond our present skills and knowledge to put right. Human resources are simply not enough and to have no other resources is failure indeed.

The world is waiting for the Christian Church to proclaim a risen Lord who is alive and active in human affairs.

But we make excuses! We say we haven't the gift; we haven't felt an imperative call. But to say this is to make too easy an escape from such a clear challenge, and I wonder to what extent our shyness to meet the challenge of Christ's commission really lies in our unwillingness to be obedient? It would be glib and untrue to say that obedience is easy. It asks for courage, confidence and trust; it asks for compassion and a deep humility. But it is worth the cost, for if our Lord's commission to his disciples is still valid for his Church, so is his promised power. Healing is not some extraordinary function by extraordinary people inside or outside the church. When a group of compassionate men and women meet in the name of their Lord, not only does he keep his promise to be with them, but such a group may quickly become a therapeutic community. Others soon feel the influence of that caring atmosphere and before long the local church is aware of a new dimension in its pastoral caring. When that is encouraged by the minister, his own pastoral understanding is wonderfully deepened. Prayers become more positive and expectant and it is a humbling and glorious experience to see prayers answered as this promised human/divine partnership becomes a reality.

It is a joy to meet old friends who knew healing years ago in the past and whose lives have taken on a new meaning as they have discovered the healing Lord. A man and his wife, members of a former church, had been among our valued friends for many years. The wife was suddenly struck by severely disabling arthritic pains in all her joints. Her doctor prescribed treatment which included pain-killing tablets. The pain remained and soon she could not turn over in bed, or dress, or rise from her chair without assistance. Her feet and ankles were swollen and walking was slow and painful. Her own words were, 'I feel ninety years old.' A consultant from the local hospital diagnosed rheumatoid arthritis but did not suggest any change of treatment.

She and her husband came from Yorkshire to my home in Birmingham to stay overnight and receive the ministry of prayer. We prayed on arrival, again in the evening and before their departure the following day. By then she could walk normally, though with some pain still. A week or so later the visit was repeated, for though she was considerably improved, pain prevented her from sleeping well. After the second ministry she slept well and the swelling in fingers and ankles disappeared; there remained only occasional twinges in the shoulders. In one month all pain was gone. In the meantime her doctor had arranged for a visit to another consultant in rheumatology who said, after examining her, 'Whatever you had has gone!' He took a blood sample to determine what kind of arthritis it was and whether it was likely to recur. The sample proved to be clear and the specialist said he could only conclude that she had never had arthritis. She, however, is in no doubt about her healing nor does she doubt that it was Christ who healed her.

This healing ministry has its true place within the normal life of a normal church congregation, for healing is at its best when it involves the whole people of God. I have found three methods helpful in developing my own ministry over a quarter of a century or more.

A vestry hour
The minister will find it of inestimable value to set aside time when people in need may talk with him confidentially. For want of a better name, I have called this time a vestry hour. It may involve a ministry of counselling or comfort or advice – or all three. Above all, it must be a ministry of prayer. To lay hands quietly in prayer upon one who is depressed or fearful or in pain may well bring Christ's healing in a few minutes. So often a sense of

48

burden is quickly lifted or pain is eased or banished and a new hope floods the soul. Such a moment can be the starting point of a changed situation or, when confession has been spontaneous, of a new beginning. This personal ministry deserves priority in the church's calendar.

Prayer groups

A prayer fellowship is a great asset both to the minister and the church. I have already referred to the therapeutic value of a dedicated praying group of men and women who feel led to this compassionate caring. Such a group will normally strengthen its own life and purpose by studying the scripture – especially the healing works of Jesus and the disciples – and will support the minister by praying daily for him and his work. It will lovingly welcome those who need 'support' as they pass through illness or breakdown. This is the Christian church reaching out to help in a loving and practical way. Care must be taken that such a group never conveys a 'better than you' impression. Compassion and humility should mark all that it does.

Healing services

Some people do not find it easy to approach the minister personally in a 'vestry hour'. Many will not feel free to turn up at a prayer group. So a third, and useful way, of reaching out to people is through a healing service quietly advertised. I am not happy about blaring publicity. Let the service be an act of quiet worship, meaningfully dealing with Christian wholeness and offering the laying on of hands to those who wish it. Some who are shy or unaccustomed to such services are able to remain 'comfortably unnoticed' as part of a larger congregation. Many, in this way, discover the reality of healing prayer. Some will discover for themselves a new and exciting content to the Christian faith and some who have come to scoff will stay to worship. It is no light thing to bring needy men and women into touch with the living Christ in this way and it is obvious that careful and prayerful preparation is needed for these services.

A time of fellowship with refreshments after the service helps to lower barriers of shyness and encourages friendships. Some who have received the laying on of hands will value this opportunity to meet and talk with the ministrant.

· The value of such an after-service fellowship gathering was made abundantly clear when I visited the Channel Islands in 1979 on a 'teaching' mission to the United Reformed Churches. As part of the programme I led a healing service on a Sunday evening and after the service we had refreshments and fellowship in the church hall. At this service there had been a lady who when she was born had been blind in one eye, and had very little sight in her other eye. Several unfortunate mishaps which led to retinal detachments later made her disability more severe, and she needed the support of a guide dog.

During the service she received the ministry of the laying-on of hands and almost immediately her sight was restored in one eye and she was able to read small print on the special hymn-sheet. Those who were there may well remember different aspects of that evening, but Barbara recalls the sense of the presence of God which she felt as a hand lightly touching her shoulder, with a restful voice saying, 'Barbara, you are healed.' As hands were laid upon her, she felt a sensation of a band around her head and of an inward washing by a flow of warm water. It was after the service that we felt her excitement as she came to me and said she could see which women had hats on. A little later, she came again to say that she could now see what colour the hats were. Copies of my book were on display and her minister took one and asked her if she could read the wording on the cover. She not only read the title, but the inset quotation which is in very small print. We certainly said 'Thank you' to God that night.

Her minister tells how her life has now changed. Improved sight has enabled her to gain an 'O' level in English, a St John's first-aid certificate, a Pitman's audio-typing certificate and a Royal Society of Arts certificate in English language. She is now working full time, and to her great delight has been allowed to keep her guide dog as a pet. She became a member of the church on confession of faith, and her minister wrote to me, 'She is the best missionary we have.'

The Church's ministry of healing and medicine

Heaven surely blesses the relationship between the Church's ministry and that of medicine. The two disciplines are complementary and need not be in conflict. To seek medical help does *not* show lack of faith in God. On the contrary, it is grateful acceptance of one of God's great gifts to this world. The Christian must thank God for every discovery made for man's benefit, for the skill of the doctor and surgeon and the insights of the psychiatrist. Human knowledge is a gift of God. So let skill and knowledge, compassion, faith and prayer join hands in fulfilling the commandment of our Lord, to preach the good news and heal the sick.

The unhealed?

The criticism is sometimes made that those who are not healed when they seek the Church's help lose their faith in God, but I have never found this to be so. On the contrary, I have many times seen prayers answered in very helpful ways, even when healing does not come. It may be true that the over-zealous in this work will make promises they have no right to make – for it is God alone who heals. And of course it is true that in the Church's healing ministry, as in medicine, some people do not respond in physical improvement when we feel they should. We have much to learn. There must be spiritual laws about which we now know little but which will one day be revealed to us. This should not make us lose heart. The gospel has the last word and it is full of encouragement.

Even in terminal illness there is a gracious ministry to offer which goes beyond mere comfort, though that is valuable enough. The prayerful approach often eases pain and lifts deep fears. It is healing in a very real sense when the sick man is freed from pain-racked hours and days, and, no longer needing sedation is able to share his last hours with his loved ones with a clearer mind. Not the least important part of the healing work that is our heritage is found here. We surround our loved ones with prayer and see those prayers answered as they slip quietly away – without pain and without fear – to the adventures that await them in a new world. Thanks be to God!

He has anointed me

Georgina Edwards

Georgina Edwards is a pen name used for this contribution
by a well-known writer.

The dullness of the day could not dim how I felt. I stepped out from the Richards' garden straight on to the sloping silver sand. The soft sand got into my shoes as I slithered down the slope – it was uncomfortable, but it didn't matter. It would have done earlier in the day, but not now.

I had spent the day with them, to get to know them, and to hear at first-hand Mary's story of healing. She and her husband, Stanley, had met me at the station, and driven me to their shore-side home. They had always lived at this sea-side resort. John, her son, had been born there, and with his wife had come down with me on the same train. He is now an Anglican minister, a writer and teacher on spiritual healing, or as he insists on calling it, 'The Church's Ministry of Healing'. On the train I asked him whether his present involvement in the healing ministry arose from the experience the family had had when his crippled mother had been instantly healed, and whether he was a 'healer'. His eyes twinkled – he didn't want to satisfy my curiosity by anticipating what might naturally emerge when we all met together.

After lunch we moved to the front room overlooking the sea. One never quite knows what to expect when meeting people for the first time. I was struck by their unity, their fun and their total lack of any sort of religious 'style' or false religious behaviour. I spent half the meal 'in stitches' as the anecdotes – many of them arising from John's ministry – flew back and forth.

54

Mary, now in her sixties, is still a beautiful woman, silver haired and with a sensitive, smiling face. She is a quiet-spoken person who, I imagined, would find sharing one-to-one in the setting of her home and family very much easier than 'giving a testimony' to a group. I asked her how her trouble first started.

'I was sixteen, and saw a very bad accident, and immediately afterwards boarded a tram. I was standing by the opening, and I must have fainted. While the tram was going full speed, I fell off and rolled into the side of the road.'

'Were you rushed to hospital?' I asked.

'Well, no. In those days one didn't really rush off to be X-rayed in the way we do today! I came round, and was taken home. I was not immediately crippled, but it was a condition that slowly grew from that time.'

'What were the indications that things were going wrong?'

'I was home and suffered from shock for a considerable time, and was in bed. The doctor visited regularly. After that, when I was up and about, I noticed that I was less and less able to walk; swimming became impossible. I was treated for arthritis of the spine with heat treatment and manipulation. This went on for a number of years.'

'John hinted to me on the train earlier that the pair of you had quite a time of it at his birth . . .'

'Yes,' she said as a mischievous look passed between mother and son. 'I was advised not to have a child – advice which I ignored! We had quite a time of it. John took three months to regain his birthweight, and was at the beginning 'dead' for a record time! We'll skip the other details! I was unable to lift him, or bath him, or, later, to push him in a pram – my mother had to do this for me.'

I felt like asking whether she regretted having him, but the father's comment in the story of the Prodigal Son sprang to mind – 'This my son *was* dead – but is alive again' – and I knew it was a foolish question.

Knowing that Mary was finding it difficult to talk about herself, her husband took-up the story.

'Mary always covered-up her suffering, and did everything possible not to be a nuisance to other people, or to let them know. Only someone living as close to her as I was knew what she really went through.' After a pause, in which he seemed mentally to be choosing what to select, Stanley added, 'She rarely got to sleep because of the pain. When she was in bed, she was often unable to turn-over without first waking me and getting me to help her. You see she couldn't allow anything to touch her back, which meant that she couldn't lie on it! It was a complex event for her even to get into a bed. It sounds incredible, but if she turned her shoulders her hips would not follow, but had to be turned by hand!'

I looked at Mary, who was for a moment back in those times, and the remembrance of the pain showed for a moment. She looked up with a changed expression. 'It all sounds a bit morbid. I went up-and-down, I had my *good* days. I could sometimes drive . . .'

'On a specially built car seat!' interrupted John quickly, knowing that she was about to gloss over the pains and the difficulties.

'When John was about four,' Stanley continued, 'Mary built him a little snowman. That was a mistake! It took two hours for her mother and me to undress her, since we could only move her limbs an inch at a time.'

They anticipated that Mary would be confined to a wheelchair and so they moved to a more suitable house. Medicine brought relief during these years, but when a doctor offered an operation on her spine that would have made Mary totally stiff, they refused that. Later their doctor – of the famous Bodley-Scott family – advised against all further treatment. It was at about this time that Mary went for an X-ray to a London hospital, but she was unable to be moved to the right position on the table for it. Her spine, to use the Richards' family term for it, was 'like a question mark' for the left hip was right out of position, and there was a bump, the size of a hand, towards the base of her spine. This was not only untouchable but was always immensely hot.'

'For how many years were you like that?' I asked.

'Twenty-eight,' she said after a moment's thought.

'Then what happened?'

This seemed like John's cue to take-up the story – 'The curate of our church was a chaplain of the local large hospital, and was known to exercise the church's ministry of healing,' he said.

'You mean he healed people?' I asked. 'Yes,' he said, hesitating, 'but I wouldn't quite put it that way . . .'

I let him continue.

'He used to pray for people and they would often get better. I remember him showing me a beautiful letter written in immaculate copperplate writing by a man whose hands had been crippled of arthritis . . . but we'll never get to Mum's healing if we chat about those stories! The time came for him to leave the parish and move north. Dad suggested to Mum that she should go to see him before he left.'

He paused.

'What was her response?'

John looked thoughtful. 'You may find this difficult to understand,' he apologised. 'At first she refused, and her reason – which, as a family we have often talked about – was basically that she was contented. She was happily married, and I was alive, and had had since the age of nine a call to the priesthood. She felt that her life was complete. She used to spend her hours in quiet inner thanksgiving to God for himself and his goodness. It sounds like some sort of religious escape or as if we are seeing the past in some rosy light! But that is how it was.'

'What changed her mind?'

'We did!' added Stanley quickly, with a knowing look at John. 'She had grown up disciplining herself not to trouble people and assumed the same relationship with God! 'I don't feel the need to bother him about something so small!' was her response. John and I said, 'But God is generous!' and persuaded her to see the minister concerned.'

'Did you doubt God's ability to heal you?' I asked.

Mary looked at me in such genuine astonishment that I felt a little foolish. 'But God *is* GOD,' she said simply, as if that answered everything – and I suppose it did.

'Did the minister have healing services?' I inquired.

'Oh no. I simply asked him to see me. The practice among the early Christians is described in the Epistle of James –

'Is any one of you in trouble? He should pray.
Is anyone happy? Let him sing songs of praise.
Is any one of you sick?
He should call for the elders of the church
to pray over him
and anoint him with oil
in the name of the Lord.'   [James 5.13–14]

'This letter of James,' John added, 'was written to members of the Christian Church, and this passage is about the Church's ministry to its own members. Jesus is called "Christ", meaning God's Anointed One. The oil symbolises a Christian's unity with the living Christ and this is why I stressed that it was a ministry which only has its fullest meaning within the *Christ*-ian family,' he said, stressing the first syllable of 'Christian'.

I was grateful for his explanation, but I was eager to hear what had happened, so I was pleased when Mary continued the story. 'I called for him, and he pointed me to the teaching of the Scriptures, along the lines that John has just done, and by way of preparation he told me to spend several days reviewing my life, one period at a time, to see if there were any areas of unforgiveness, any unhealed relationships, any resentment I was hanging-on to, or bitterness, and so on. The purpose of that sort of exercise – which can itself be very painful and costly – was, I think, to "clear the decks" so that God could work as freely as possible in my life.'

'Do you think that such a preparation was important?'

'Yes I do,' she said without hesitation, 'although God is big enough not to depend on our general spiritual state before he will do something! We'd prepare our homes and hearts if royalty were coming . . .'

'On the day, I went with Mum to the minister's home. I always walked at her side taking one arm, and we went up the steep rockery steps to his front door. The welcome and the home was very quiet, and orderly. There were no hearty greetings, or casual chat, or coffee. We moved to his front room in which he had placed a large armchair for my mother to sit in, another chair to the side, and, simply laid out, a small table prepared for a Holy Communion Service: bread, wine, and in addition, a small bottle of oil. It was more like a cross between a hospital and a church sanctuary than what some today would call a "healing service"! Mum had always insisted on kneeling when she went to church (although it sometimes took weeks to get over it) and this was going to be no exception.' He chuckled. 'We got her to her knees, and wedged her between the two large chairs.'

'Were you prepared for this service?' I said, not quite sure what I should ask at this point.

'Yes,' she replied, 'being Anglican it was totally predict-able . . .' we all enjoyed the joke, '. . . at least, as far as the service was concerned!' When she said this she produced a small booklet giving the 1936 suggested form of service for the Laying-on of Hands and the Anointing of the Sick. I looked at it briefly, but, wanting to hear more, I thought it could keep until I was on the train home.

'What were your thoughts as you came to the service?'

'I was praying for John,' she said, somewhat surprisingly.

'Yes,' John added by way of explanation. 'I'd injured my back playing left-prop in rugger at school, and Mum's main concern was the healing of my back!'

Although I knew I was delaying the climax of the story, I wanted to ask . . . but John looked at me, shook his head, and mouthed, 'No it wasn't!'

'Were you thinking of yourself at all, Mary?'

She looked thoughtful, 'No, I don't think I was.'

'The service – there must have been something extraordinary or special about it . . .' I was groping for words. An Anglican service taken from a little blue book is not what I imagine as a spiritual 'high'! Was this going to be the climax to what I did know was a very remarkable healing! I asked about its content and what the clergyman did.

'It was the same as any home Communion Service for the sick,' explained John, 'with Scripture readings, prayers, an opportunity to say "sorry" to God and to receive his forgiveness. The sick person and other Christians present receive the bread and wine, which, you'll remember in the Prayer Book words, are for the preservation "of *body* and soul unto everlasting life" So the Communion Service is always in some sense a healing service.'

'What about the minister?' I asked, as I sought some outside sign of spiritual power.

'He took it like any other minister takes a private Communion Service in a hospital,' came the accurate but, for me, slightly disappointing reply.

'May I say something?' John asked. 'The presence of God is not either increased or guaranteed by the fuss we make about it. In fact his presence is often more real, and he is freer to do great things, when we are quiet before him, and stop making a religious racket. This was that sort of occasion. The minister took the short service, anointed my mother with oil on the forehead, making the sign of the cross with his thumb, and prayed –

'. . . I anoint thee with this holy oil, that thou mayest receive the anointing of the Holy Spirit, unto the healing of all thy infirmities of soul, of mind, and body."

'The oil,' John continued, 'is an outward and visible indication (like a wedding ring) of something that is not visible. The prayers of the service make that distinction – which is a necessary one if we are not to think that in some way the oil is magic. Listen to this –' He borrowed the little book from me, and quickly finding the place read,

'"As with this visible oil thy body is *outwardly* anointed, so may our heavenly Father grant of his infinite goodness that thy soul may be *inwardly* anointed with the Holy Spirit, and be filled with all strength and comfort."

'You could anoint someone outwardly with oil until the cows come home, that does not bring healing. The healing is the invisible action of God which the oil symbolises.'

John seemed quite at home with such sacramental acts, and what he said made sense, although I had not heard it put that way before.

'What happened at the end, or after the service?'

'The minister had arranged things so that we didn't go off into social chatter. He simply went quietly out of the room and left his front door open for us to leave when we wanted to.'

'During the service,' Mary continued, 'I was so aware of the presence of the living Christ, that I knew that if I looked up I would see Him! I was aware not only of a healing, but of a deep, deep, *cleansing*. The healing I experienced was a very painful manipulation as God put my back in place, it was almost like being ground into the floor! I was literally pushed back into place again! No person was even touching me at the time! It wasn't a gentle soothing away of pain, but a ruthless and painful reshaping, as,' she added reflectively, 'so much real healing often has to be. John and I stayed kneeling side by side for some while in the quiet . . .'

John burst in, 'My eyes were shut in prayer as I knelt there, and I heard a faint rustling next to me. I looked to the side – and there above me – Mum was *standing*!

'We left very quietly, and habit made me prepare to help her negotiate the steps. I moved to take her arm gently, and hey presto – one, two, three, four, five – she was down the flight of steep steps! Yet she could never manage stairs before! She looked up at me with a radiant face. "You know what's happened?" she said. "Yes!" I exclaimed.'

'Did you shout from the housetops?' I asked.

'No, the very opposite. Mum said to me, "Let's not make a fuss, I don't want to make a fool of God, let's go home quietly."'

I was puzzled, 'What do you mean "make a fool of God"?'

Mary said thoughtfully – 'I was aware that we can imagine or feel great changes when we are touched by an atmosphere of prayer. Had I in some way made myself feel better, consciously or unconsciously, it would not have lasted. Had I shouted from the housetops that God had healed me – and he hadn't, I would have made him appear a fool. Perhaps I expressed it badly then, but I wanted to safeguard against my imagining things, and behaving in such a way that would dishonour God.'

John resumed his account. 'We went home and spent the day quietly in order not to move out of the experience of God's presence that he had given us.'

'The next morning was really something,' Stanley burst in. 'Mary had slept the whole night through. I had never

* My own experience on Sept 16th 1985

known this and I called John. It was so obvious to us that my wife had been completely healed, that we got her to stand by the bed, and she stood absolutely straight! John asked her to touch her toes, and slapped her hard on the base of her spine – the place that previously could never be touched!'

I tried to fight back the tears of wonder and joy that I felt, but through my own blurred vision I saw that the Richards couldn't keep back their wonder either!

I didn't feel able to speak, so I totted-up the length of time since that service – twenty-five years.

'Has there ever been any recurrence, or back pain of any sort during those years?' I asked.

'None whatever,' they said almost in unison.

It took me some while before I could decide on my final question.

'What was the first great new thing you did, either by yourself or as a family?'

John answered. 'My parents had always lived by the sea. From the time of her accident in her teens, my mother had never been able to walk on the sand. The first thing we did as a family was just that – we walked for the *very first time* as a family along the beach.'

Time was pressing; and the interview had to end there. I had a train to catch, and they offered to take me to the station.

I looked out of the window towards the beach. As if reading my thoughts, Mary said, 'You can either catch the bus right outside, or walk to the next stop via the beach.'

I left them.

My day was no longer dull. I walked on the sand – and it was good, very good.

Christ the prime mover

Reginald East

The Rev. Reg East, formerly warden of the Barnabas Fellowship in Dorset, is author of *Heal the sick*, which was written to encourage Christians, ordained and lay, to take the healing ministry 'into their system'. Here he tells how he sees Christ, the prime mover, preparing the way and leading in the ministry of healing.

It was about 8.45 on Sunday morning. As I left church after celebrating at the Holy Communion Service, I felt a strong inner urge to visit a parishioner, one of our local dustmen, who was in hospital. Sunday was a busy day with at least five services, so it was not until after Evensong that I could go to the hospital, though the urge to visit this man had increased as the day wore on. When I arrived in the ward the sister asked, 'Have you brought his wife with you?'

'No,' I replied, 'Should I have?'

She then said they had sent for her because it was thought he would not survive the night.

I went to the man's bedside. The bed was curtained off and a young West Indian nurse, who was in constant attendance on him, told me that he was having repeated fits. I enquired if she was a Christian and when she replied that she was, I asked her to pray with me as I laid hands on the patient. After prayer I returned to the ward sister and there found the man's wife. She was in a highly emotional state. We did our best to comfort her and after a time I went back to her husband. The nurse told me that the fits had now ceased. So we prayed again, and soon afterwards I left the hospital. Early next morning I telephoned to enquire about the condition of the man. The sister replied, 'You'd better come in and see him again; you've done him some good.' When I arrived, he was sitting up in bed having a cup of tea and smoking a cigarette. In due course he was transferred to a London hospital where an operation was performed and after some months he was fit enough to return to normal work.

The healing of this man is, incidentally, an example of the benefit that comes from co-operation between the medical profession and the Church in its ministry of healing. This is going on continually, though often unnoticed. Every now and again one has such an example of an immediate or almost instantaneous healing, but usually healing is a process lasting days, weeks or even months.

At times God does not give physical healing but can soften and beautify character through the experience of illness. Some people are taken into the mystery of suffering. Because of sin, suffering is an integral part of life and none of us escape it completely. The cross is the centre of Christ's redemptive act, and we all have to understand something of the cross if we are to enter the new life which Christ offers to us. Illness leads many people to a deeper understanding of the cross and of their redemption in Christ and this of itself brings joy and spiritual healing. Christ also takes people to himself through death. To a Christian death is not an evil thing, nor is it to be dreaded. Some of the most lovely experiences of my life have been to see gracious souls, full of the light of Christ, depart joyfully into Christ's nearer presence.

The healing described above happened at an important time in my ministry, for though I had seen God heal on other occasions, the force of the inner prompting of the Lord meant that he was the prime mover, directing the events. It reinforced my conviction that what we call the healing ministry of the Church is in reality Christ himself continuing his own ministry of redemption through his Church. He is still completely involved in the world, sharing humanity's joys, sorrows and suffering.

In another gracious act Christ showed me not only that he was involved in our lives, but also that he was well aware of what was necessary for a full healing. One evening a man telephoned to ask for prayer. He had a bad heart and this condition was causing him particular distress because he was relatively young. We prayed together over the telephone for some minutes. A few days later the following letter arrived. 'Many thanks for the telephone ministry the other day. Immediately after I put down the receiver I was overcome by a tremendous overpowering emotion from the depths, in which all my failure and sin came pouring out, and all I could do between sobs was to tell God that I was a failure who had treated him like dirt, and ruined the creature he had intended. For years I have been aware of a large dead area which knew nothing of God, and I had prayed that he would deal with it. I had forgotten that I had made that prayer! Anyway, the upshot has been that my heart quietened down almost at once, and the dead area is now alive; for the first time I can accept my failure, because God does, and really feel forgiven. I am no longer quite literally breaking my heart in the depths of myself. I have had a medical examination, and everything is normal.'

What a marvellous work of love that was by our Lord. It again shows his total involvement in the human situation. Though the man was concerned primarily with his physical condition, Christ dealt with the basic problem, thus making possible the healing of the body for evidently the illness was caused by the man's spiritual need. Again, it is clear that Jesus not only commands us to heal but is himself actively engaged in healing. The infant Church understood this, for they prayed, 'And now, Lord, look upon their threats, and grant to thy servants to speak thy word with all boldness, *while thou stretchest out thy hand to heal*, and signs and wonders are performed through the name of thy holy servant Jesus' (Acts 4.29–30). It is noteworthy that in the incident just described healing was made at a distance. It shows that the Lord is active everywhere and that healing does not necessitate the laying-on of hands or anointing, though such ministry can be an encouragement to those who are sick.

As the ministry of healing developed, I found that God cared for people of all ages, even quite old people. Usually one would not expect healing of an old and worn-out frame, but in his compassion Christ may give old people his healing touch. I remember well a lady of eighty-eight. Her home had been burgled and the shock had brought on double pneumonia which caused her diabetic condition to get out of control. I laid hands on her in hospital and she experienced what she could only describe as 'light'. Within two days the pneumonia had cleared up and the diabetes stabilised. The nurses in the ward called her 'the miracle lady'. Another old lady said to me, 'It's when you lay hands on me that keeps me going.' It helped her to keep her independence.

Young children respond well to ministry, probably because faith has not yet been undermined by doubt and disappointment. At a holiday conference at Whatcombe House a couple came with their little boy. He had been a normal healthy baby, but at the age of twenty months he had had a severe gastric upset from which he had not had chance to recover before a second bout of diarrhoea hit him. As a result he could not tolerate milk in any form. After six months the parents were referred to University College Hospital where, after numerous tests, the only hope that was offered was that he might grow out of it. Tests had eliminated certain possible causes: his absorption of fat was adequate, there was no intolerance of lactose, neither was he allergic to any of a wide range of foods. Nevertheless, the child could not tolerate shop bread, cake, biscuits, sausages, some forms of baked beans, many sauces or a wide variety of tinned goods. Fruit and vegetables had to be used with caution. After nearly two years of this, the parents had begun to lose the battle to keep up the lad's protein and calcium intake and his growth rate was slowing down.

By the last day of their stay at Whatcombe House the

condition of the boy was, if anything, worse and the father asked for help. We laid hands on him shortly before the family left for home. Some time later the mother wrote to say that on the following day, the diarrhoea had cleared up, even though he had been allowed some butter in his diet. He was put back on milk, nearly a pint a day, and since then there had been no further negative reaction and the boy had been able to eat normally. Three months later, at the next routine visit to hospital, he was discharged. He had shot up two inches within a month of going back on milk.

In a very large proportion of cases, physical illness is the result of emotional or spiritual disorder. Asthma, digestive and bowel problems, heart and skin conditions, rheumatism and arthritis, are often indicative of deeper trouble. As we minister to people with such ailments, paying attention to underlying emotional and spiritual conditions, we find that the physical manifestations can disappear. This leads us into the area of much of our Lord's deep and lovely work – the whole realm of emotional or inner healing. Because of a whole range of factors very many people today are finding life too demanding. Consequently, in order to keep going, they resort to mild drug prescriptions from their doctor to relieve depression, strain, anxiety and an inability to cope.

Christ shows his healing power with many people who are in such a state. Help is asked by people who are depressed, who feel unloved or unwanted, who are not ill enough to necessitate hospital treatment, but who find, nevertheless, that life has lost its joy and purpose. They feel inadequate or useless, often under par, and plagued by anxiety, worry, fear or guilt. This leads to inner loneliness and difficulty in relationships. In large numbers of cases in which I have been privileged to share, I have seen God bring people to an inner peace which has enabled them to resume life in a more positive and fruitful way. Here is an example of the healing of a lady who had quite a lot of inner suffering, described in her own words.

'I was born in May 1945 and have a sister eight years older. I lived in a family which was generally opposed to religion, and where violent episodes due to overdrinking were prevalent.

'The story of my healing begins in October 1973 when I found faith in the Lord Jesus Christ through deliverance from evil spirits. (I had been involved in the occult for a number of years, hoping to find a meaning to life.)

'I had been ill since January 1970 with a complete breakdown, and for nearly four years I had undergone various forms of medical treatment, culminating in a period in a psychiatric hospital where I underwent narcosis (sleep therapy), all to no avail. For the period during the breakdown I was taking thirty-four pills a day, including eight 5mg of Valium, three of Nardil and fifteen of Inderal (the latter were to steady my heart which on occasions was beating two hundred times a minute). Among the symptoms I experienced were many phobias, a feeling of strangulation – a persistent lump in my throat – pressures and tightness in my chest and stomach. Most days I had at least one panic attack in which unknown fears completely overwhelmed me.

'Life became totally unbearable and I often considered suicide. I was away from work as often as I was there, and eventually had to resign my job as well as withdraw from all activities outside the home. My marriage was on the rocks. I was a medical write-off, at twenty-eight years of age.

'When I accepted the Lord Jesus Christ into my life that evening in October 1973 (incidentally my husband did so at the same time), I found a meaning in life, and very soon, in consultation with the doctor, I could radically decrease the number of tablets. But after about eighteen months, having stopped taking all the tablets except about 10mg of Valium, I was unable to cut down any further. After much prayer with our vicar and his wife as to why I was making no more progress, we were led to receive deeper ministry and in March 1976, with my husband, I went to Whatcombe House where we were introduced to the ministry of inner healing. On a number of occasions over the following months I was ministered to in a very deep way during which the Lord through his Spirit, took me back to areas in my past which needed his healing touch, including trauma during the birth process. This ministry revealed, among other things, that I had buried very deep anger against members of my family, especially my mother who had overprotected me as a child. My father had died in 1967 and I had never been able to express my grief at the time.

'As the areas of deep pain were exposed to Christ's healing love, the symptoms gradually disappeared – the lump in my throat was the last to go. The number of tablets I took diminished further until I was completely free from each and every one of them in July 1979, and today (two and a half years later) I am still free of them. During the past year, the Lord has helped me shed four stones in weight, much of which I had put on during the illness.'

This lady and her husband are now themselves involved, in their parish church, in ministering to others who are in bondage to the emotional pains of their past.

There were some quite disturbing elements in this lady's background, some of which have not been mentioned for family reasons. While a surprising number have such traumas, many people from all levels of society who need inner healing come from what we would call a normal background. That is to say, their parents cared for them, wanted to be good parents and provided what they considered to be a family life that gave more than the necessities of life. Nevertheless the children have grown up with problems. In the final analysis it transpires that they feel they were not loved for themselves. The cause of this is that in some way the parents, or other adults involved, had been unable to make a true relationship with their children. This may be because of the parents' emotional difficulties, for example, the mother's emotional needs may drive her to try to possess her child. Post-natal depression can cause a rift between mother and child, as can the removal of a baby from its mother for medical reasons. Or some mothers for whatever reason, may say that they are unable to bear the thought of having another child. All these and other factors can cause a child to feel it is unwanted. Similarly, fathers play their part. Someone will say to me, 'My father was a retiring person,' which means that he could not relate to his children, or 'I felt that father's first love was his work. The family seemed to come second.'

I have seen our Lord enter into the inner agony of many, giving them a new sense that they matter so that they have been able to accept themselves. As a result, their attitude to life has blossomed. While many people have been released, it must again be said that, for reasons which could not always be found, others have not come out of their prison. There is no magical or automatic action by God and in areas such as these with so many complicating elements, one may suffer the disappointment of seeming failure. But even in such cases, the willingness to share another's pain can never be in vain.

Sometimes the Holy Spirit leads us to the sources of problems by showing us pictures (or visions) or giving us special 'words of knowledge' about someone's condition. When this happens it confirms to me again that it is God who is directing and controlling the healing. I remember at a conference there was a lady who was on leave from abroad who asked for ministry. As I prayed, a picture was given of a flower in full bloom which began to shrivel. I mentioned this and she replied, 'That is a picture of myself. My spiritual life *has* shrivelled and I feel empty and lost.' As we continued to pray the Spirit said that there were three things which were the cause of this condition: a sexual problem, a deep guilt, and a fear. We were then able to deal with each of these as she admitted them and through counsel and absolution she came to an inner peace and knew again the presence of God. God then said, 'She can be filled with the Spirit.' So we prayed and the Spirit filled her soul. I had a message from her two years afterwards saying all was going well.

So I believe in healing because God has made it abundantly plain to me that this is not the fad of a few cranks, but that he, himself, is active as he has always been, in caring for those he has made. One joy is that he is strongly active 'At such a time as this', when the need is so great, for church after church is awakening to this realisation and one sees the ministry of healing becoming an integral part of their life.

Cure and healing

Ruth Fowke

Dr. Ruth Fowke is a consultant psychiatrist in South East England. She is the author of *Coping with Crises*, and is a popular conference speaker. She brings to this subject a wealth of insight gained from her knowledge of the Holy Spirit's work in inner healing allied to her professional expertise.

As a doctor I am trained to alleviate distress of mind and body, and to promote cure where it is at all possible to do so. As a Christian doctor I have the privilege of working with others in pointing people towards that wholeness of being which is what I understand healing both to achieve and to be. We humans cure, only God can heal, and this distinction is important.

I believe that healing is very much more than the removal of symptoms, however welcome that relief might be. To understand the distinction, consider the common problem of toothache. To have that gnawing pain removed is a wonderful release but it is at best only of temporary and dubious benefit unless the decaying process that causes the pain is also halted and its effect remedied. Until this happens the tooth will be left in a weakened state and will one day crumble, unable to cope any longer with its usual tasks. The ache can be cured by various means but it is all too likely to return unless there is considerable remedial work done on the diseased tooth, and the sufferer may also need to alter his habits if he is to prevent a similar problem recurring in the future. It's no use having only the necessary fillings, he ought to stop chewing so many sticky toffees, eat more apples, and otherwise modify his previous practices.

Cure is removal of the pain, healing is about removing the origin of the pain and altering the habits that encouraged it to grow. It is concerned with remedying the dis-ease in our very beings and may include a reversal of disease processes, putting right that which has gone wrong over the years. It reaches to the depths, the core, the very essence of our being and changes us so that we cannot be the same again. The practice of medicine cannot renew a person, it can only repair or restore function; but healing changes him. Unless we are prepared for change, prepared both to be changed and to change our ways if necessary, it is no use looking for healing. The penetrating and pertinent question, 'Do you want to be made whole?' gets to the heart of the matter. Unless that invalid (John 5) had been prepared to face a different sort of life, prepared to change and to begin to do for himself things which he had formerly left to others, he would not have received his healing.

The change that is necessary for healing can be instantaneous, which is miraculous and miracles, by definition, are rare. On other occasions the time normally required to achieve change is speeded up but it sometimes takes place almost unnoticed over a period of time. Speed is not the important thing; to become whole and healthy is the goal. In this age of instant everything, from coffee to cookers, our concept of healing tends towards the 'instant' variety. In our impatience for the end product we discount and devalue the idea of a process which is changing us and which in turn requires us to alter in response to the changes which are being worked out within us.

When ten leprosy patients were cured they all lost their symptoms completely, yet only one can be considered as healed (Luke 17). Only one was changed in his inner being so that he could not rest until he had gone back to express his gratitude. He had to acknowledge the wonderful change that had taken place. The other nine were cured of their symptoms but not healed in their total being. They returned to pursue the same way of life they had always followed. Their illness was an interruption to their life-style but, compared to the tenth man, it was clearly a missed opportunity.

Even minor ailments can be an opportunity for healing in this deeper sense because they are an invitation to change from the style of life that gave rise to them to a healthier manner of living. Aspirin is an excellent anodyne for headache; it cures the pain but it does nothing to prevent a recurrence. Sometimes aspirin alone is insufficient and the sufferer may also need to stop what he is doing in order to rest for a while, perhaps having to retire to a quieter place before the cure is effected. If while doing so he reflects on the likely area or areas (they are frequently plural) of stress and tension in his life that have culminated in this headache on this particular day, and is prepared to modify any of his actions, reactions or attitudes that have made him so tense, then he is open to being healed.

Headaches and many other disorders that are symptomatic of inner stress occur because of the build-up of tension within the person, and, if recognised at all, this tension will probably be blamed on to overwork or other pressures from sources outside the person. Removing or lessening these outside pressures often provides a degree of immediate relief but long term release from the tendency to get into stressful situations will only come if the inner drive impelling a person into that particular way of life is dealt with. For instance, many people are workoholics. They either cannot delegate or, if they do, they will then take on two new responsibilities for every one they shed. This tendency to persist in trying to pour two litres into a one litre bottle afflicts many of us and shows itself in various ways but always the root of the problem lies in early, and by now quite unconscious, attitudes and beliefs. A common source is the inner, deeply buried belief that, 'I am only accepted, and therefore only loved, when I am good and live up to the expectations of . . .' This can lead to an almost compulsive need to succeed, to a fear of failure in any form, or to a life-style of intense rivalry. This latter problem is compounded by the competitiveness that rules in many schools and is continued in a large number of the sporting and recreational activities of adulthood.

Cure is the removal of such symptoms as tension headaches, compulsive work patterns and destructive competitiveness, whereas healing has a broader and deeper function and aim. Inner healing, the specific aspect of the larger concept with which I am most familiar, concentrates on dealing with the hidden roots from which these disorders arise. In theory this may be likened to a steady process of dealing first with the rootlets just under the surface. When those are cleared away bigger and deeper ones become apparent and as those in turn are dealt with even deeper ones are discovered and finally removed. In practice it is neither as rational nor as orderly.

There are many and various ways in which God sovereignly releases people from crippling, negative beliefs, attitudes and emotions, and in so doing he takes them into a profound transformation of their relationship with himself. This can be a purely private, entirely personal event, either sought after or sometimes occurring spontaneously during a time of worship and devotion. Although this may take place when the person is alone with God, it is more likely to do so in a corporate gathering, especially a sacrament that is bathed in prayer. The presence of others seems to facilitate healing, and often it is necessary for one or more to be actively engaged in the healing process, and to minister in various ways at different times in this personal but accompanied journey into the individual's past with all its hurts, hang-ups and hang-overs.

Particular wounds or attitudes are dealt with as they emerge into consciousness, or as they become evident in dreams, through behaviour patterns, by 'following the feelings' wherever they may lead, and by observation of eloquent body language. Events are not therefore dealt with in the chronological order of original occurrence but as they become accessible through one or another means.

The language of a person's bodily posture and a knowledge of likely emotional responses both contribute to an understanding of where to look for the root of the problem. For example, more was revealed through the body than by the words of the man who said he was content to remain single and to go on supporting his widowed mother but whose jaw, fists and trunk all visibly tensed whenever she was mentioned. Another man, deliberately sent to a different school than the one attended by his friends, and in other ways prevented from associating with them, asserted that these events had not affected him. Later he came to realise how these arbitrary parental decisions coming on top of his earlier experiences had coloured his reactions to other people over the years, and had distorted his idea of himself as a person.

These important languages of the body and of the emotions can be studied, understood and utilised but they are by no means the only or the best tools that we have. The use of such spiritual gifts as a word of knowledge, wisdom or discernment can be crucial. We need to seek them from the Holy Spirit and to exercise them with faith, boldness and discretion in the pursuit of inner healing.

It is the memories of feelings rather than the accurate, objective facts that are important in inner healing. Sometimes it is the ability to feel again the feelings one repeatedly experienced in earlier years, and at others it is the re-enactment of the impact made by a particular experience that opens the door for the healing of those bad times. When they are recalled and relived there is the opportunity for Christ, who is timeless, to enter into those felt experiences and by his presence in them to restructure the memories. In this way the person becomes released from their negative effect on him, free now to grow, free to develop his personality without the restraint of those earlier wounds.

It is the dimension of prayer and the exercise of sovereignly distributed Holy Spirit gifts given for the occasion that enables healing to occur in ways and at levels quite innaccessible to secular therapies. Many of these can uncover past wounds, unravel complexes and accurately discern the inner plight of people, but none known to me have the power to undo the past, to transform the tangled web woven deep in a person's history and to remake an injured personality – in short, to redeem the person. To pretend that they can is presumptuous, but to discard them because of their limitations is surely equally unreasonable.

I believe we need to work for a truly functioning partnership of all that modern medical practice has to offer, utilising sound psychological principles and working with the rich, though often neglected, resources of the Church. Healing is not the exclusive domain of either medicine or the Church, rather it is a joint task in which both disciplines complement each other.

One of the crucial factors in healing is the ability and the intention to forgive. Most of us know that if we want to be forgiven we must forgive others. 'Forgive us our trespasses *as* we forgive others' is in the universal family prayer. It is also true that if we want to be healed we must forgive because until we do so we will be hanging on to strong emotions that harm us both physically and psychologically. When we are unable to acknowledge and deal with anger, resentment and bitterness towards others we ourselves will suffer. These powerful emotions, when locked up inside us, cause tension which results, amongs other things, in muscle spasm as well as an upset in the finely tuned chemical regulation of body and mind. Our skin is often the mirror of the mind, we blush when embarrassed, go red with rage and white with fright. However hard we may try to conceal what we are really feeling, reactions like this accurately portray what is going on inside.

When we say, and mean, that we have forgiven someone for the hurt they caused us but still go tense at the mention of their name then our body is betraying our lack of true forgiveness. It seems that there are several stages to work through before this healing state can be achieved. Our initial reaction to an inner injury is likely to be either a denial of feeling hurt at all or a declaration of forgiveness that remains at head level only. It does not involve the heart and therefore does not heal. When we get over the denial and acknowledge the hurt, we also need to admit to the anger, hostility, bitterness or other feelings it arouses in us. Having admitted to that, we are then likely to go through a stage of bargaining in our minds with the one who has injured us. We say, 'If only he will admit he's wrong, then I'll forgive him', 'If she will say sorry then I'll talk to her again', 'If he will stop drinking (smoking, swearing, staying out so late) . . .' This 'if' shows how conditional is our attempt at forgiveness. When we realise this we will probably have to struggle with ourselves and may become downhearted in the process. If we persist in facing the full impact of the hurt, and can acknowledge our own responsibility to respond with unconditional acceptance of the person who hurt us, then we are almost there.

Forgiveness is not complete until relationships that had been broken by injury are repaired. When there is this reconciliation the individuals concerned are released into a new freedom with one another and within themselves. Forgiveness that is healing does not consist of overlooking, forgetting or excusing an action but in facing what has already occurred, accepting the consequences and carrying on in those very circumstances. To do this is to take risks – the risk of being hurt again, of being rejected, misunderstood or misused. Without risk there is no life, only an existence governed all the time by fear, and there is certainly no healing without some risks being taken.

Another aspect of healing that is frequently overlooked is the element of suffering that may be an essential part of achieving this eventual goal. When anyone goes into hospital for a planned operation, walking in fit and well, apart from some natural apprehension, they are prepared to put up with the discomfort and limitations of the immediate post-operative period in order to have a higher standard of health afterwards. They know that they cannot have this without going through the temporary distress that surgery entails. Even in these days of wonder drugs, medical treatment usually takes rather longer than surgery before the patient feels the benefit. Mental and emotional conditions require not only more time but also a greater involvement of the person himself with his own progress. There must be a willingness to take the risks of living, and to suffer a bit in the process in order to feel better later, and to be able to cope more effectively with the problems of life as they continue to occur.

Life will never be without problems of one sort of another. Indeed, sometimes people find illness less of a problem than health, especially if they have had that illness for a long time and have become used to the way of life which it imposes. They soon find that they are required to do more for themselves and to take on more responsibilities when they are well. Being able and willing to accept the proper demands of life is one of the necessary outcomes of healing. This, together with suffering so often involved during the process of healing and the time taken to grow into wholeness, are aspects of health that are generally unwelcome and disregarded.

If people are to be able to stay with the pain and then take on the responsibilities that come with healing, they need the care and encouragement of friends who will stay with them in their journey into wholeness. The best environment for healing is the local church when it is really being a caring body of believers who can accept the dark side of people, and accompany them in their distress, instead of trying to chivvy them out of it prematurely. We need to combine acceptance of the person where he is on his own journey at this moment with the expectation that he can change and that healing him is within the power today of our sovereign Lord God.

Many agencies are concerned with the cure of symptoms, and in particular we must note that spiritual sources other than the divine may be called upon. When this is done cure can and does result but true healing will in fact be hindered rather than helped because occult and psychic forces are opposed to the holiness of God. Beware! Those who invoke them, or receive their help, are led away from, rather than led into, the wholeness of God. The current upsurge of interest in these psychic and occult forces in the pursuit of health is a measure of our failure, as Christians, to 'preach the Kingdom of God and to heal the sick' as Jesus specifically commanded his disciples.

Emergency into light

Pam Moore

Pam Moore is a wife and mother who has known a long, brave struggle with depression. She tells with honesty and courage of her gradual healing.

'Help me – Oh God, please help me! Do something, please . . .' The cry hit the white emulsioned walls and bounced back from the Artex ceiling. No gossamer-winged angel came to my side. No voice from heaven spoke words of comfort. No loving arms encircled me. There was only the silence; the fearful oppressive silence hanging in the air which moments before had resounded with my cries and the hammering of my fists against the door. The God who promised never to leave me nor forsake me appeared to have done just that. The everlasting arms had dropped me.

What had gone wrong? From the age of twelve, when I had made a definite Christian commitment, I believed I had been building my house upon the rock. Believed that Jesus was changing me. Believed that the years of prayer, Bible-reading, involvement in the church, witnessing, fellowship and seeking to be obedient to God had been leading me into a relationship with him that would see me through anything. In theory my house should not have fallen down. In practice there was no denying that it had. And great was its fall.

People said to me, 'But there's no reason for you to have had a "breakdown". You have a lovely home, a wonderful husband and two delightful children – what more could you want?' My family, upset and mystified, asked the same question, adding, 'and nothing has ever happened to cause this trouble.' I had to acknowledge the truth of these statements, with guilt and misery. I could not relate my condition to a nightmare childhood nor to later experiences guaranteed to crush the most valiant of spirits.

On the contrary. My life had been built on a respectable middle-class foundation: devoted parents, a good education, material comfort, reasonable healthy and, most important of all, strong Christian principles. My own Christian commitment had been made shortly after the conversion of my parents and elder sister through the ministry of Dr Billy Graham. From then onwards family life had been centred on personal and corporate Christian activities. Generally I conformed willingly and enthusiastically to the expected Christian conduct, even in the usually rebellious teenage years and in the face of 'temptations' at College. The strict code of Christian behaviour gave me security and my adherence to it served as a mask for my unease outside Christian circles and my fear of anything new or challenging.

I rejected my chosen career in journalism on the grounds that it would be too tough for someone of my disposition, and began training for social work. I enjoyed my job, but my health was affected by the stress of travelling long distances in an unfamiliar area and living alone in a bed-sit. I had severe panic attacks and could not eat. By this time I was engaged and the wedding date had been fixed. I gave up my job and returned home to be knocked into shape for the great day. In March, 1966, Robin and I were married, amid much pomp and ceremony. Robin was not only a Christian, he was kind, capable, hard-working, good-looking and came from a background as impeccable as my own. How could we not live happily ever after?

The panic attacks subsided with the termination of my job, but they had brought long-standing misgivings to the surface. Originally I had been drawn to Jesus because I had so many fears and I heard of his love for me and his longing to help me and be my friend. Once I became a

Christian, though, my relationship with Christ became an affair of the head rather than the heart. There was much dwelling upon sin and repentance, of telling others about God's love, demonstrated by the death of his Son upon the cross to purchase their salvation. While I shied away from any form of religious emotionalism, I feared that my intellectual evangelicalism would not sustain me in a time of real crisis or tragedy when I could not give up as I had done with my job. I could only wait and hope that in such circumstances I would receive the assurance I needed.

The birth of our first child, with his near-death and subsequent bouncing-back-to-life presented us with the crisis, but not the re-assurance. The cheerless hospital ward offered little comfort, I felt terribly alone, and the sensation of being cut off from God added spiritual torment to the considerable physical and emotional distress.

The failure of my faith in that situation was exposed when I was asked to give a Mothering Sunday talk describing how being a Christian influenced the early days of motherhood. Suddenly my feelings erupted in an angry outburst followed by tears. I declined the invitation, sobbing out the sorry story and adding that being a Christian made things worse. God demanded our love and obedience, but what did he care about exhausted parents, let alone a screaming baby who would not feed or sleep? At last I had expressed my real feelings! It was painful, but also a relief. Over the next two years I slowly recovered as a result of talking with our minister, prayer for healing and release from fear, and some basic psychotherapy arranged by my doctor. Robin and I believed that we had emerged from the experience stronger and wiser.

The birth of our daugther sometime later was straight-forward, and there seemed to be no reason for the dead-weight depression that set in some months after her arrival. The depression varied in intensity but never lifted. The continuing feeling of rejection by God in-creased the misery, and while the experience of baptism in the Spirit led my relationship with God into a new dimension, the depression remained. But so did the promises of God. There surely had to be some way of escape from darkness and despair, if only we could find it!

Our search took us to a Fountain Trust Conference and our first encounter with 'inner healing'. There was a talk on depression and Robin arranged for me to see the speaker. I reacted violently when he asked me to describe my childhood: after all, it was post-natal depression that was causing the trouble! 'I had a happy upbringing,' I protested, 'nothing wrong . . . if you met my parents . . . just tell me why, when I'm supposed to be a mature, intelligent person, I feel like a four-year-old . . . wanting to be loved . . .' He appeared to draw his bow at a venture but the arrow was right on target as he replied, 'Because deep inside you are, still, a child.'

He gently led me to a level hitherto unexplored, and during the course of an afternoon he encouraged me to talk about events in the past, re-living them and letting out the emotion blocked off at the time of their occurrence. These memories were then re-recorded, bringing Jesus into them. I was sure that we were on the right track, in spite of being drained by this ministry. It was difficult going back home. I had been expected to find help at the Conference, and the 'help' I had received was viewed with scepticism when I did not immediately recover from all symptoms of depression. If anything, I appeared to be worse. I was no longer imprisoned by the cold numbness, but my release was not into a state of tranquil normality. Instead, all the emotions of childhood began to come to the surface, and they were increasingly difficult to disguise. I was told by my church that I was a bad witness and would put people off becoming Christians. It seemed as though God was rejecting me through his people, and I felt hurt that I had only been wanted by him and by the church while I was able to be good and useful. My condition was labelled variously as sin, demon-possession, immaturity, and attention-seeking.

We floundered on. My relationship with Robin was under considerable strain, and we clung to various conferences and the people there who were able to offer some help and succour. One summer holiday we went down to Whatcombe House, where we found a haven and committed support. Life became more stable. By expressing my feelings in lengthy letters and phone calls to members of the community, I began to enjoy a much more settled daily life. If only those hundred miles were not separating us from the people of God in whom we had found our refuge and could put our trust!

It seemed like a miracle when Robin's job took us to Dorset. After months of long-distance caring, suddenly we were going to be living within a few miles of the community. It seemed as though God was leading us out of Egypt, at last.

In spite of the ever-present cloud of tension and depression many things had been changing. My strictly academic background, so in keeping with all that was sensible and reasonable, was giving way to the development of creative activities. I had always day-dreamed about writing, art, and music, but had never done very much to make them a reality. I was encouraged by the fluency with which I was able to express my feelings in poetry and letters. I developed a new interest in music, took up piano lessons again, and learnt to play the guitar. All this conflicted strongly with the attitudes instilled at school and home, but I discovered that I felt more confident and more at ease in these areas than I had ever done with secretarial studies, a degree in Economics, or dusting!

We settled quickly in our new home, and found a church in a neighbouring village where we established an instant rapport with the minister and his wife. I vividly recall writing our Christmas cards just four months after we moved, describing how wonderfully God had prepared our path. Away from fears of disgracing my family, and the pressures of a church's expectations, we could look forward to re-gaining our confidence, and emerging into a new way of living.

Only weeks later our confidence was shattered. Our new way of life took an unexpected and bitter turn as anxiety and depression came creeping back. In spite of the doctor's reassurances and tranquilisers, the symptoms began to increase rapidly. I had thought that the emotions of the past six or so years had been intense, but these feelings swamped me. Just before we had moved I had an unpleasant virus infection and the move itself had been demanding. I no longer had any strength to fight the pounding waves that buffeted me. Again I sensed terrible isolation from God. My belief that I was, over the years, being transformed into the likeness of Christ collapsed as, terrified and in despair, I wept that I could not go on. My inability to pray and my newly acquired fluency in swearing surely confirmed that I was no longer a child of God. How short had been my sojourn in the promised land.

My doctor contacted a Christian psychiatrist, and I received out-patient treatment at the local hospital. Treatment consisted of talking about my anxieties and discussing different aspects of my life, finding anti-depressants and tranquillizers that suited me, and narco-therapy. The psychiatrist explained that drugs were unlikely to provide a complete answer, but would give support while I found a way through the problems.

Once again we had the experience of being dropped by a church. Once again Whatcombe House picked us up. The members of the community had all been away on extended leave during these difficult weeks, but when they returned and learned what had happened, Reg East offered to take me on. My psychiatrist knew of Whatcombe House and felt I could benefit from their help. Arrangements were made for me to go there at regular intervals as soon as I was stronger, and thus it was that I had the privilege of receiving ministry from someone for whom I had the highest regard and in whom I had complete confidence.

In common with others, Reg East believed that the early years held the key to the mysteries of the emotional turmoil, and he picked up the threads of that first experience of inner healing. While he was always understanding and accepting, our sessions were definitely structured and were hard work, for I was expected to co-operate with him in my own healing, under the direction of the Holy Spirit.

This involved the exposing of hidden hurts, and opening them up to the healing power of God. As deeply buried feelings rose to the surface I was encouraged to take Jesus into the dark places and let him work in these areas. This was not easy. My expressed desire was to 'not be', and plots for escaping into oblivion figured prominently in my thinking for a long time. Healing came second to that, and even if I could have been promised instant, painless wholeness I would still have opted for a way out. I was carried along by the faith of others, and their vision for me – and Reg East's constant exhortation to 'go bravely on'. I have gone on, though not very bravely.

How I would rejoice to proclaim that the years of darkness are now behind me and I have emerged into dazzling sunshine and a perpetual foretaste of heaven. How thrilling it would be to announce that the re-building process is producing the turretted fairy-castle of my dreams, with St George ever-present to slay any advancing dragons! How I long to declare that my relationship with God is made up of joyous days walking hand-in-hand with my Father, and nights of respose as I lie at peace in his encircling, all-protective arms. The reality is not like that, but maybe miracles are not always obvious, dramatic, or in accordance with our own desires and designs.

Perhaps it is a miracle that the anxiety, fear, panic and depression have not been allowed to destroy me, and that progress, albeit very slow, is taking place. Depression still causes me to nose-dive. Panic reactions still frighten and hinder me. Anxiety and tension still rob me of peace. But less and less do they govern my life, dictate all my actions, and dominate my thoughts.

I can manage day-to-day duties more easily: getting up in the morning, taking the children to school, shopping, cleaning the house, preparing meals. There are times when I do panic about such things, but I no longer wake up every morning with a thudding heart and a sense of dread, wondering how I am going to drive less than a mile to school, or go to the shops without being overcome by nausea, dizziness or trembling.

I have begun to make friends, and to talk freely with them on a variety of topics, neither fiercely trying to avoid the subject of depression, nor dwelling on my despair and failures. I can go to church, out to tea, even to parties and meetings now, without being acutely aware of a feeling of isolation as though I am imprisoned in a transparent box, a small child at a grown-ups' gathering, gauche, ill-at-ease and lost.

Rather than rebelling against my dependence on drugs and feeling guilty that I have to rely on them and not on God to give me peace, I am trying to see them now as his gift to us. The process of finding tablets and the right level of dose is a difficult one, as one after another tablet produces unpleasant or distressing side-effects, aggravating the original problem. I am so grateful that for the time being, at least, a particular combination of tablets seems to provide a generally good state of stability.

My relationship with God has moved on from the tormented one to which it had plummeted. I am still cautious, and find it difficult to trust. I still feel confused about how to interpret the promises in the Bible, and how to decide whether something is from God or from my imagination. I have never stopped believing in God, only in my capacity to relate with him and to grasp spiritual matters aright. Robin and I can now pray together most mornings, just simply and briefly, and for the most part I can enter into that. The times when it produces angry and frustrated reactions are getting less frequent.

As a wife and mother I feel less of a failure as my confidence has begun to grow. I don't feel so swamped by the domestic routine now that I have outlets for creative activities. I had the opportunity to help at an art class for the elderly, and after two years of assisting in a voluntary capacity I was invited to take over as official tutor. Teaching was one of the things I had never seen myself doing, and I protested that I had neither teaching nor art qualifications! This objection was dealt with by the suggestion that I should take a teaching course, which I embarked upon, confident that a couple of weeks would prove my ineptitude. Somehow I kept going, always on the point of giving up, always nervous of the drive to college, always convinced that the particular piece of work I was doing would be my last. I ended up with a distinction, and am now teaching one morning a week . . . art! I still can't quite believe it. I also attend adult education art classes as a student, and find this another satisfying means of self-expression. In art, music and writing – all at an unspectacular level – I feel that I have an identity of my own and can be myself. This seems to have a spin-off into the other areas and I do not have to struggle all the time to be the sort of wife and mother that from somewhere I have got the idea that I should be. I seem to be less swallowed up by the emotional and physical demands of these roles, and therefore better able to cope with them. Gradually I am feeling more part of our family, rather than an inadequate outsider trying to fit in. The outside activities are not an escape route into which I channel all my energies – I have more interest and concern for home and family now (I still hate dusting!).

These examples do not seem very earth-shaking, and I recognise that there are still areas where I have a long way to go. But in the darkest days I never envisaged even getting this far. It has been, and still is, a struggle. Often I have felt alone, but in fact I have not had to fight by myself. There have been many hurts, set-backs and disappointments, but I have also been loved in ways that I had dreamed of, but never thought I would know. Some very dear and special people have battled with me and for me, and Robin and the children have stuck with me. I cannot, at this point, describe the quality of this love, or its full meaning to me, as I do not think that I recognise and appreciate it yet. I can only say that it is very beautiful, and my gratitude cannot be adequately expressed. I have seen the love of God in the eyes of these people, I have heard his words in their voices, and learned something of his care, strength and protection in the warmth and shelter of their arms.

Some lines by Robert Browning have been a great encouragement to me over the years, and they have a message to all who enter the blackness.

> If I stoop
> Into a dark tremendous sea of cloud,
> It is but for a time; I press God's lamp
> Close to my breast; its splendour, soon or late,
> Will pierce the gloom: I shall emerge one day.

So be it. With God there is always hope.

Moving the mountain

Jim Glennon

Canon Jim Glennon of St Andrew's Cathedral, Sydney, has for twenty-one years been conducting a healing ministry. Central to this is the congregation which meets in the Cathedral every Wednesday at six o'clock. His book *Your Healing is Within You* came out of the experiences of this congregation. Here Canon Glennon writes of his own breakdown and the healing which led him into this ministry.

'Is there anything you can learn out of all this?'

That was the one question I had not asked myself. Times without number I had gone over in my mind all that had happened. I had looked at it from every angle and weighed up every factor. Not that it was difficult to see where things had gone wrong; it was a case of strain being added to strain until I had broken under the pressure. As a social worker, I knew the questions to ask: perhaps that was the difficulty – I thought I knew it all. Not that my training had prepared me for what breakdown really meant. That was a strange new world no textbook could describe. It was more than strange; it was frightening; it was horrific.

When there is a real break-down of ego-functioning, you become a different person to the person you have been all your life. There is something of the Jekyll and Hyde about it. The new you is different and unpredictable. You have new motivations, but lack the old restraints. On the surface you try to appear normal, but underneath you are a pack of ravening wolves. Fear grips you because you can't always control them. They break out and you are 'different'. Friends and acquaintances are mystified. You would like to explain, but what can you say? If you don't understand something yourself, it is no good trying to unravel it for someone else. That is when you ask question after question; but there are no answers. For me it was the dark night of the soul.

I could blame other people for the circumstances that brought about my trouble, and this I did not a little. The devil of resentment is that it is justified – at least, we believe it is. There is a natural tendency to 'pass the buck' and leave someone else to hold it.

When everything was as bad as it could be, when there was nothing left to draw on and nowhere else to turn to, something happened that changed my life. God spoke to me. The Holy Spirit said: 'Is there anything you can learn out of all this?' The words were formed in my mind in an indelible way. I can remember them as though it was yesterday. Nothing like it had happened before. Some people affirm that they have a kind of 'hot-line' with God. I am not one of them. But on this occasion I knew the reality of hearing the voice of God. Since then, over the past twenty-five years, there have been four other times when the same kind of thing has happened, and all of them have been times of extreme need. As far as my experience goes, it is when I am at 'the end of my tether' that God is strong in what he says and does.

As I have said, it was the one question that had not been asked. It had never occurred to me that there was something to *learn* from all my difficulties. I could but listen. He went on straight away, 'You are to learn to depend on me more.' When the Holy Spirit speaks, you not only know what he says, you also know what he means. Both the message and the meaning were crystal-clear to me.

Before this time, when I prayed about my problems, it was with the idea of God helping me with them, and I always added, 'If it be thy will'. Whatever else this did, it did nothing for my problems; they only got worse until I could not carry on. Something else that was said in church circles to those in need was, God's 'grace is sufficient for you' (2 Corinthians 12.9, RSV). I didn't minimise that, but this verse seemed to be used as a substitute for doing something which would actually make a difference to the burden being carried. Frankly, I don't think the church knows much about drawing on God's help so that the circumstances of life are changed in a tangible way. It does no more than employ a community resource with 'amen' on the end, and has a theology that is a 'let-out'.

But now, despite breakdown and all that it meant, things were suddenly and wonderfully different. In a moment of revelation, a whole new understanding had been given on how I was to react to my circumstances. Despair became hope, fear became faith, and my arm was strengthened for whatever lay ahead.

The problems were still there, but they were no longer 'rubbing me out'. Now they were to do something for me: they were to become the reality with which I was to depend more on God. It was a kind of transposition – one thing became another. Instead of my God helping me with my difficulties, now my difficulties were helping me with God. It was a turn-round. Before, God was (as it were) behind me and I was looking at my mountain. Now it was the mountain that was behind me and I was looking at God. It meant that instead of my homing-in on my problems, my problems were to enable me to home-in on God. This was what I was to learn; this was what I was to do.

When you are in the middle of a wood, you don't come out straight away even when you have (at last) got on the right path. And I was in the middle of my wood. Everyday I had to discipline my prayer-thinking so that the permitted difficulties in my life were changed from loads to be carried into lifts on which I turned to God, and moved towards him until I depended on him in mind and heart. It was a tremendous relief at least to know what to do, and I persevered with it until it came out right.

I continued in prayer until I was inwardly and meaningfully depending on God alone. When that position was reached, I experienced a deep, quiet oneness with God that was all-pervading. If, after I was resting in the Spirit, a problem slipped around the corner so that it began to worry me again, I would put it behind me and come back to affirming my oneness with God. In the best sense of the word, it was putting the positive in place of the negative. The next day I went through the same procedure again.

It was never easy, and I frequently got it wrong. One of the things I learnt was that it was vital to begin the day right. It was no good starting off with a worry session or a hate session and then trying to come to joy and peace in believing later on. Neither could one wait for one's more formal time of prayer before beginning to pray. The pressure of my old anxieties was still heavy upon me, so I had to affirm my dependence on God before I was out of bed and continue to affirm it while brushing my teeth, and driving my car, and keep it in a corner of my mind throughout all the day's activities. Not infrequently it meant holding on for dear life, reiterating my dependence on God every moment of the day without so much as putting in a comma. This was no virtue on my part: I got it right because there was no alternative; it was a self-survival exercise.

It might help if some more detail is given as to how I went about doing this. It was one thing to know *what* to do and another to know *how* to do it. Well, I learnt by trial and error. The really important thing was to fill my conscious mind with the presence of God. So I affirmed that reality in a present-tense kind of way and kept on affirming it. I took a phrase that expressed this and said it silently or out loud and over and over again. 'Father, I turn to you and fill my mind with your presence. Thank you that you are with me now . . .'

One thing led to another, and I then began to emphasise that fear does not come from God. He has not given us a 'spirit of fear, but of power and of love and of a sound mind' (2 Timothy 1.7, AV) . . . 'love casts out fear' (1 John 4.18, RSV). Instead of affirming fear (which was what I had been doing up till then) I dwelt on the power and love and soundness of mind that he provided for me and wanted me to have. My affirmation went something like this: 'Thank you that you want me to have these good things. I am drawing on them now and believe it by faith.'

What helped me most was to praise God. Because I was depending on God; because he was giving me power and love and soundness of mind; because what had been revealed to me was being put into practice; I praised God. 'Thank you Father, thank you Jesus, thank you Spirit. Thank you for what you have done for me on the cross, thank you for what you are doing for me now. Praise God, praise God, praise God . . .'

Sometimes a problem came into focus that was so much a problem that I was unable to turn to God. However great my need of God, however much effort I made to reach him, I came back to affirming the difficulty and to being swamped with self-pity. I exhausted prayer and prayer exhausted me. When this happened, there was no alternative but to let the problem ride. At a later time I would return to it again, and find that my prayer reaction was then more effective. It was as though the earlier prayer effort had taken me along the road some distance, despite having come to a stop. When I started again, it was from the previous stopping place, and further progress was made. Even so, exhaustion point could be reached again. But if I persevered, I found in the long-run that I could react to any mountain in the positive way I have described.

As I came to the inner reality of depending on God and getting it right, if not every day, certainly in a general way, two things happened. The first and most important was that *the Holy Spirit showed me more of what God was like*. Words cannot convey what this meant. All that can be said is that it was a new and wonderful experience of being guided into the Truth. The things that were highlighted were specially to do with the holiness of God, and my duty and privilege to draw on that wholeness for myself and be made more and more like him. It was both elevating and humbling to be ministered to in this way. This gracious work of the Spirit did not come to me every day, but it came two or three times every week.

One of the memorable aspects of this experience was its perfect development. It was a growth experience. Each revelation (if that be the right word) was complete in itself, but was also a needful preparation for the next one. The next experience, when it came, built perfectly on what had gone before. An analogy, which is an unworthy one, is that it was like going on a journey and coming to a breath-taking view that had not been seen before. Then you turn the next corner and there is more.

This leads me to say that at a later time I realised that everything shown me was in the Bible. It took some time to see this, because it was all so new and different. I had read the Scriptures for many years and treasured their truth in my heart, but can only say that when the Holy Spirit causes the Truth to be truth for you, it is as though you had never heard it before.

The second thing that happened was *my lifelong problems began to disappear*. This part was not so easy to assess, because as they disappeared I forgot what it had been like before! It was as though they had never been. When Jesus spoke of the mountain being cast into the sea, he used a figure of speech that describes exactly what takes place. With me, the mountain was moved spadeful by spadeful. It took a period of three to four years, but moved it was, and never to return. The only time those problems ever come to mind is when I deliberately recall them to give a testimony of what God can do when we draw on his help in an effective way.

At the time I thought of these things as problems that were being worked through. It was only later that I saw that my 'dark night' with its good end-result was an echo of what Paul the Apostle had himself gone through. It was fascinating to realise that as he worked through his own crippling difficulties, he too was overwhelmed by them at first and only later saw their religious significance. 'We should like you, our brothers, to know something of what we went through in Asia. At that time we were completely overwhelmed, the burden was more than we could bear, in fact we told ourselves that this was the end. Yet we believe now that we had this experience of coming to the end of our tether that we might learn to trust, not in ourselves, but in God who can raise the dead' (2 Corinthians 1.8,9, Phillips).

The problems don't come from God; they come from Satan and the sin of the world. But they work together for good because God uses them to serve his good purposes. Paul said that the good they serve is to bring us to the end of our tether, that we might learn to trust, not in ourselves, but in God. Although it had taken me a long time to get the message, and then only because of intervention from above, this was what I had begun to do. I didn't call it healing, but it was the foundation on which healing was later to be built. More properly, it could be called a theology of permitted difficulties.

As I got on top of my own permitted difficulties and grew in this scriptural understanding, to my surprise people began coming to me asking for help with difficulties of their own. I was surprised, because people had not sought me out before in this way, and because my experiences had not so far been shared with others. My visitors just came 'out of the woodwork'. With hindsight I realise that God had sent them. He uses us according to our capacity to minister help and healing, and we comfort others with the comfort with which we have been comforted by God.

Not that I had any real idea how to go about this, but a knowledge of counselling procedures gave me a start. I accepted these people, listened, and sought to understand. When it came to doing something to assist them, I just told them what God had done for me. We were to learn from our difficulties so that we depended on God more. If they got that principle right, then everything else would come right. Although individual circumstances varied greatly, I found that anyone who followed the guidelines that have been set out drew upon the same power with the same remarkable results. Men and women increased in their experience of God, and in varying but meaningful degrees left their presenting problems behind. In other words, this wasn't something for me only, but was for all those who would apply it in their own lives.

One thing more needs to be added. As my understanding of these things grew, I found the real need was to seek God for himself. Even when we turn to God and depend on him more, our preoccupation can still be with ourselves and our pain and our burden. That is not wrong in itself and is more than understandable. But if what has been said is to work in an optimal way, we have to come to the point of wanting God for himself and not so that he will cast our burden into the sea.

No one says it is easy; but if we set our hearts to understand and grow in our capacity to do it, we will ultimately want this more than anything else and rejoice in it. And when that happens, the heavens open and we cannot contain the blessing God pours out. God is no man's debtor; if we seek his kingdom and righteousness *first*, then he meets our other needs as well.

Ultimately we should thank God for our problems, because without the motivation they give we would never come to the good things that can be ours when we react in a positive and creative way. The strange truth is that through our permitted difficulties we come to the power of Christ, and by the power of Christ our mountain is moved. St Paul summed it up superbly, both for himself and for us: 'I will all the more gladly boast of my weaknesses that the power of Christ may rest upon me' (2 Corinthians 12.9, RSV).

This has been my story of these things.

Healing and medicine – complementary?

Nigel Dale

Dr. Nigel Dale, for some years a general practitioner, is an Elder of a London house fellowship and the area secretary of the Caring Professions Seminars, founded to provide a Christian voice in the professions, and to give pastoral support and encouragement to those who work in them. He writes of the relationship between God's healing and medicine.

I was just beginning my second year as a medical student and God had been opening up to me the reality of the working of the Holy Spirit. The meeting was in a small hall in West London. The evangelist was in full swing. Around me, people were being healed from all manner of illnesses; that is, they were if I could believe what they were saying. And it certainly seemed authentic. 'Well,' quipped the evangelist, 'if there are any doctors here, they could be out of a job after tonight.' He wasn't being serious, but his words hit me with tremendous force. What was God saying to me? Why had I, a very junior medical student, come to this meeting? Where did medicine fit in, if at all, when God was so obviously able to intervene in the lives of people in direct and supernatural ways?

The reality of healing had been shown to me a number of years before. I had been a typical Christian teenager wanting to serve God and to have my own way in life. Suddenly, the Lord broke in by healing me clearly and directly of a severe case of hepatitis. I knew that it was the Lord. Yet in the busyness of my life the incident passed over without really affecting me. However, in the back of my mind, as I prepared for medical school, there was the knowledge that Jesus heals today, not just in New Testament times.

In the Bible Jesus' healing miracles seem to occur for a number of reasons. The first, and perhaps the clearest reason, expressed in Matthew 8.17: 'He himself took our infirmities and bare our sicknesses', is his great willingness to heal all those who have been brought to him. The writer of this Gospel clearly understood that the atonement of Jesus on the cross as foretold by Isaiah referred not only to Christ carrying our sins but also to his carrying our sicknesses. Jesus was the living expression of the redemptive nature of God. This is shown in one of the seven great covenant names of God: Jehova-Rapha (see Exodus 15.26), 'I am the Lord that healeth thee'.

The second reason why Jesus performed so many miracles, was his great compassion for the multitudes coming to him (see Matthew 9.36).

The third reason was to authenticate the Gospel. In John 10.37–38 Jesus explains that he must be doing 'the works of his Father'. He challenges the people that even if they do not believe what he says, they should believe the works that they can see.

There is little to suggest that the miracles of Jesus were unique. We see similar miracles, both in terms of power and scope, in the Old Testament, and in the life and works of the apostles and others in the book of Acts. We do not know that Jesus cured everyone instantaneously and completely, and that there was no recurrence of disease. What we do know is that he healed all who came to him. But stories such as the healing of the ten lepers suggest that whereas they were all healed, only the one who came back to thank him, was made whole. Some would understand this to mean that although all ten had the disease process exterminated only the one thankful leper actually had the deformity corrected and was brought back to a place of wholeness. On another occasion when Jesus prayed for a blind man, it appeared that the man's vision was only improved. Jesus then prayed again, leading to a restoration of normal vision. I am sure this does not suggest in any way that Christ's power is limited; rather if teaches us that in some situations we may need to persevere in our praying (Luke 18.1–8).

In Matthew 10.1 and Luke 9.1 we see Jesus delegating his healing ministry to his disciples. He subsequently gave a very similar commission to the Seventy (Luke 10.1). The wonderful results of this commission in the life of the disciples and in the Seventy did not stop with the earthly ministry of Jesus. As we go on into the book of Acts we see healing brought not only by the apostles, but also by Philip the evangelist. The apostle James, in fact, commands the elders in the local church to be willing to pray for the sick and tells them to expect the Lord to raise up the ill man (James 5).

Jesus who is 'the same yesterday, today, and forever' is still moved with compassion as he sees our physical and mental needs. It seems inconceivable that what he did before the Cross should be terminated now that we have actually become partakers of the New (better) Covenant.

F. F. Bosworth, in *Christ the Healer*, writes: 'The word "soteria" which is the Greek word for salvation, implies deliverance, preservation, healing, soundness, and in the New Testament is applied sometimes to the soul and other times to the body only. The Greek word "sozo" translated "saved" also means "healed", "made sound", "made whole". In Rom. 10.9 it is translated "saved" and in Acts 14.9 the same word is translated "healed" referring to the healing of the man lame from birth. The Greek words for "salvation" and "saved" mean both spiritual and physical healing.' Dr C. I. Schofield in his footnote on the word 'salvation' says, 'Salvation is the great inclusive word of the Gospel, gathering into itself all the redemptive acts and processes.' This word must certainly include, for our possession and enjoyment, all of the blessings as revealed in the redemption of Christ.

It seems to be indisputable that Jesus wants to heal, and that he wants to heal today, so where does the art and science of medicine fit into the picture? To clarify this we need to establish in our minds the difference between the workings of God within the creation and the direct intervention of God that supersedes the natural laws that he has established and maintains. God is a 'God of order and not of confusion' (1 Corinthians 14.33). Without this, certainly, science and medicine would have no basis on which to work. We see in the orderly and wonderful ways in which God has created this universe a pointer towards the living God (see Roman 1 for Paul's exposition of this argument). But the creation does not reveal the personal Christ who died for us. To come to know God *personally* we need to come through the mediation of the Lord Jesus Christ. In medicine, too, we can see the laws of God in the reliable way drugs work or in the marvellous way that the body heals itself following illness and injury. The workings of medicine are a part of the 'common grace' that God bestows on all men. He 'sends the rain on the righteous and the unrighteous' (Matthew 5.45). Likewise, Christian or non-Christian physician working alongside the laws of God will see the same results. However, it does not follow that 'healing of body and mind has been delegated by God to trained physicians by advances in medical knowledge and technology' for God is not bound by the creation that he has established. He is far above 'all rule and authority and power and dominion' (Ephesians 1.21). He can *actively* intervene to super-naturally bring healing when it is sought by the prayers of his believing people (see James 5.16; Mark 16.18, etc.).

Some of the above can be illustrated from an experience that I had while working as a junior houseman on a surgical firm. We had had transferred to us from another hospital a young girl who was suffering from recurrent bouts of severe abdominal pain, followed by black-outs. These had been extensively investigated by us and by the previous hospital, but with no clear cause in view. The consultant pyschiatrist had seen her and felt that she was mildly depressed, but accepted this as within normal limits considering her condition, and the recurrent pains that she was experiencing. The consultant surgeon in charge of the case was a devout Christian. Though we followed the laws of medical science to the best of our ability we were not able to get to the bottom of this young woman's illness. As the young girl was also a Christian the consultant suggested finally that my wife and I might like to take her to our home for a few days' break from the hospital. As we shared our home with her he thought that the Lord might give to my wife (also a doctor) or myself some wisdom as to what was going on. This we proceeded to do. The young lady had been with us for a few days when the Lord spoke to my wife during prayer that she needed to ask the girl if she heard voices. As soon as an opportunity presented itself we asked this question and she replied, 'Yes, but they have told me not to tell anyone.' So, a part of the problem was out. Further questions uncovered the following remarkable story.

About the age of fifteen, she had suddenly begun hearing 'voices' while she was in classes. These voices became more and more insistent and menacing as the months went on. So to get rid of them she developed the knack of having severe bouts of abdominal pain followed by the black-outs. These pains and black-outs were real enough for her to believe them to be real, as did everyone who examined her. Only when she blacked out was she able to 'black-out' the voices. Constantly now they were telling her that the only course of action was for her to kill herself. They told her that 'they' would kill her if she told anyone of 'their' existence.

In spite of our awareness of how most psychiatrists would understand the girl's situation, we felt that this story had one probable interpretation. Demonic spirits were plaguing this girl to seek to destroy her. Jesus said such things are the essence of the work of Satan (John 10.10): 'The thief comes to steal, and kill, and destroy – I came that they might have life, and might have it abundantly.' This girl needed that 'life'. So we bound the spirits in the name of Jesus, and commanded them to leave her, and she was set instantly free. She has remained free to this day – approximately five years after the event. The glory goes to Jesus for his great power.

It is worth noting to whom the glory goes in most instances when people are healed through the competence of dedicated physicians. The credit goes to the physician, even though he knows that, at best, he is aiding the natural recuperative powers of the body in its fight against disease. But when the healing comes from the supernatural intervention of God then the glory must go to God for it is in this situation that one is made to think on the things of God.

There is a beautiful example of this in the healing of the blind man by Jesus in John 9. The Pharisees (verse 24), trying to trap the man who was born blind, tell him to 'give the glory to God'. What they do not realise is that this is exactly what the blind man is doing. He knows that it is through the direct intervention of Jesus that he has been healed. So in giving the credit to the person who healed him he was giving the credit to God. This is not the situation, though, when we give the credit to the physicians, who, though they may be commended for their genuine efforts, are not responsible for the actual healing. God will not share even a little of the glory that rightly belongs to himself with any other (Isaiah 48.11).

A distinguished Christian physician told me that a child had been brought to see him privately who was in the advanced stages of a type of leukaemia. Although the finest treatments available at the time had been given to the child, he had not responded, and was becoming dangerously ill. This doctor encouraged the family to pray. He also prayed for the child and laid hands on him, as was his practice with the patients that he felt the Lord wanted him to pray for. To everyone's delight the boy rapidly began to improve. He then lost contact with the family for over a year. When he next heard from them they wanted to ask his advice. They were so thrilled with the way that the boy had recovered after seeing him that they wanted to give a large sum of money, not to the Lord, but to medical research at the hospital that had been treating their child. This doctor felt really grieved that they were in effect giving the glory to man when he knew that the child had actually responded to the healing power of Jesus. I have found this in my own experience: people try to give us the credit for what God has done. How important it is for anyone praying for the sick to point them towards a personal faith in God through Jesus, who is the source of the healing.

Praying for one's patients and witnessing to them raises a number of questions that many Christian doctors and nurses, among others, have not found easy to answer. Is it right to be sharing one's faith with someone who, because of illness, is very vulnerable? What right do we have to be pushing our faith on others who may not wish to hear about Christ?

To answer this we need to look at the whole question of 'mission'. Who gives us a mandate to share about Jesus? The answer must be that God does. He, in fact, 'is now declaring to men that all everywhere should repent' (Acts 17.30). When faced with the question of authority, Peter and John (in Acts 3.19–20) made it very plain that they felt they were primarily answerable to God. It is God who has sent every Christian out into the world 'to preach the gospel'. Obviously one needs tact and discretion when sharing one's faith; but this should not be an excuse to keep silent before someone with needs that we know only Jesus can satisfy.

Doctors, particularly those who are engaged in either psychiatric or general practice, find that many, if not most, of those who come to see them have disorders which find their roots in the 'psyche'. Christians know that some of these problems emanate from the spiritual, as well as from the psychological, condition of the person. One of the great weaknesses of so much medicine is that it is not involved in treating the whole person. What is going on in our spirit or in our soul affects in turn our soul and body.

I was looking after Sally while she had come as a patient on the ward where I was working. The day after admission she had had a termination of pregnancy for an unwanted baby. Now she was morose and beginning to regret the step that she had taken. As we talked together, she poured out her feelings of guilt. What should I do as her doctor: help to cover up that guilt, or point her towards a Saviour who can remove our guilt and shame? To me the answer was obvious. God had called me to minister to the desperate and eternal need of this patient, not merely to offer temporary alleviation of her guilt with a false sympathy. How glorious it was, as I shared with Sally the love of the Lord Jesus, to see her hand over her life to the Lord. A day later, while still on the ward, she was marvellously filled with the Holy Spirit as we prayed together. A boldness in witness can reap eternal dividends. The commands of Jesus provide the framework for ethical decisions.

The question of what is the genuine need of the patient is one that all doctors have to face constantly. The lonely, bored housewife; the angry teenager; the unmarried mum who is pregnant again; the frightened old age pensioner who virtually never goes out for fear of being mugged: all of these find their way to the doctor's door, along with a host of people with similar problems. Is a repeat prescription of Valium and a bit of a chat really the answer for these folk? How do we deal with anxiety: by covering over the symptoms with drugs or by pointing the patient to the real healer, the Lord Jesus Christ? He is able to come right to the root of the problem and to bring a deep healing at the source of the trouble.

Elsie came to see me in her usual depressed state. She lives on her own, with about half a dozen cats. Her basement flat in an old house reminds one of Fort Knox in the number of locks and bolts that protect her from the outside world. She feels that nobody cares about her. Last

week another of her neighbours was mugged which greatly strengthens her knowledge that this will happen to her
one of these days. 'Please may I have my usual tablets,
doctor?' The 'usual' is an assortment of anti-anxiety and
sleeping tablets that she has been started on many years
prior to my arriving at the practice. She seems to cope on
these. But this is hardly 'abundant life'. So we chat a little
about what is going on in her. I try to point her gently
towards the one who is able to bring meaning into her
rather frightening world. She begins to share some of her
problems from the past. She hates her brother for something that he did many, many years ago. She is filled with
bitterness, which has in turn given way to fear. Now she is
a prisoner of her own making, in her own home. She
knows that Jesus will give her a way of escape and forgive
her sins, but she will not let go of her unforgiving attitude
to her brother. And so, like the rich young ruler, she goes
away sorrowing. She could have had a full healing in
Jesus. Instead she has chosen to hold on to her sin, and her
tablets so that she can cope.

Another situation presents itself at the surgery which
turns out to have its roots in life situations much deeper
than at first appear. Anne has recently returned from
abroad to her birthplace in London with her two young
children. She has come back because her marriage has
fallen apart. She wants to be in her familiar surroundings
but it is not proving that easy to adjust to life here in
England.

I have only seen her in the surgery once before. This
time she comes to me complaining of pains in the neck.
Examination and investigations do not reveal much of
note, but she is obviously rather depressed. As I ask about
this, her marriage problems come out. Her anxieties over
making ends meet, seeing the children settle in to new
schools, and re-adjusting to life without a husband are all
taking their toll.

On her next visit to the surgery I begin to share with her

my understanding that there are answers to loneliness, depression and despair. She does not seem particularly open to what I share, and as I am rather busy I cut things short and lend her *Prison To Praise* to read. The next day she returns.

While with me the previous day she experienced an unaccountable sense of the presence of something (one) beyond herself in the room. She went home frightened, but decided to have a look at the book anyway. Half way through the book she just knew that Jesus was the answer in her life. She dashed out of the flat, across the road, and into a nearby church building where she threw herself down in front of the altar. There she handed over her life to Jesus Christ. Immediately she felt, to use her own words as if 'I had been taken out of a kingdom of darkness into a kingdom where everything was so light.'

It is interesting to note that the depression and anxiety are completely replaced by her new found joy. The pain in her neck does not seem to be touched at all by what has happened, but is spontaneously resolved over the next few months!

These examples from my own experience illustrate a point that has been increasingly important to me over recent years. It is not enough for us to be a witness by our example. We can point people to Christ by the way we live and the way that we work, but in the final analysis 'faith come from *hearing* and hearing by the word of Christ' (Romans. 10.17). The spoken word has tremendous effect. Invariably as we look at the Gospels and the book of Acts we see Christ and those who followed his example, not only doing marvellous works in the name of God, but following this up by the spoken proclamation of the message. The apostle Paul put it another way when he stated, 'Knowing the fear of the Lord, we persuade men' (2 Corinthians. 5.11). When God wants to communicate himself to man he speaks. His word becomes flesh through the words of the prophets, through his people, and most gloriously as the full expression of himself in the Lord Jesus Christ. 'And the Word became flesh and dwelt among us, and we beheld his glory, glory as of the only begotten from the Father, full of grace and truth' (John 1.14). When God created he spoke. 'Then God said' is not just a poetic way of expressing things, but an actual description of the way that God acts. Possibly the words that the Lord spoke to Jeremiah the prophet exemplify this when he says, 'Therefore, thus says the Lord, the God of hosts, "Because you have spoken this word, Behold, I am making my words in your mouth fire, And this people wood, and it will consume them."' When we speak on God's behalf, God acts. 'He sent his word and healed them' (Psalm. 107.20) still needs its human agency to make it real in the lives of people. We can be active channels for the grace of God, but we must be prepared to speak the word. 'Just say the word, and my servant will be healed', is the response of faith that Jesus commended so highly in the centurion.

The apostles showed the same dependence on the power of the Spirit and the word when they prayed in Acts 4, 'And now Lord, take note of their threats, and grant that thy bond-servants may speak thy word with all confidence, while thou dost extend thy hand to heal, and signs and wonders take place through the name of thy holy servant Jesus.' Can we offer any lesser prayer in our desire to see the good news of Jesus spread into the world for which we are responsible? We can respond to the challenge of the message of Jesus to bring salvation (wholeness) to the world. We can actively proclaim this glorious message to those with whom we have contact.

Scripture quotations are from *The New American Standard Bible*. Patients' names and minor details have been changed to protect their identities.

I'll cycle for God

Joyce Huggett

Joyce Huggett, author of *Two into One?*, and editor of *We Believe in Marriage*, is on the staff of St Nicholas' church, Nottingham, where her husband, David, is rector. She tells the story of Alistair Campbell.

Alistair was bored. It was Monday, his day off. But what was there to do on a wet afternoon in February? Maybe he would go to see that film which had become the talk of the town. 'I couldn't sleep for nights after I'd seen it.' 'It's horrific, it's evil,' he had been told.

Alistair, a disillusioned young man in his late twenties, joined the cinema queue where he found a group of young people distributing leaflets. But Alistair, not one to imbibe propaganda, screwed up the yellow leaflet, pushed it in his pocket and shuffled in to see the film.

The Exorcist disgusted him. He walked out during the interval, went shopping, then wandered aimlessly back to his empty flat. That evening as he thought about the film, he wondered what all the fuss was about. He remembered the students and the leaflet now lying crumpled on top of his shopping. Idly, he glanced at it.

It urged the reader not to see the film. Cinema-goers had suffered mentally and spiritually from this encounter with evil, it claimed. Because of this, a group of Christians were offering help to any who needed it. 'If you would like more information, ring one of these numbers.'

This invitation intrigued Alistair. Why should church-goers get involved? Perhaps he *should* telephone one of the numbers and ask.

He picked up the phone and dialled the first number. No reply. The second, 52646, produced a ringing tone. I answered and Alistair, now in aggressive mood, explained, 'You won't know me but I found your number on the back of a leaflet which was handed to me when I was queuing for *The Exorcist*.'

I'd heard variations of this explanation several times already in the past week, sometimes in the small hours. They were from people too disturbed to sleep; too frightened to go home to empty bed-sits.

'How can I help you?'

'I wouldn't like you to think I'm frightened,' Alistair continued. 'In fact, I found the film boring. I rang to ask you why young people from the churches spend time bothering people in cinema queues. I'd have thought there were more worthwhile things for Christians to do.'

Alistair's voice was argumentative. I sent a prayer to God while I made some quick decisions.

'Where do you live?' I asked.

'In The Park,' he explained.

'That's very near our rectory. Why don't you come to meet us and then we can chat. How about tomorrow night at eight?'

He was obviously taken by surprise.

'Yes! Thank you. I'd like that,' he admitted. 'Tomorrow at eight. My name is Alistair Campbell.'

'What kind of person is Alistair?' my husband asked later that evening.

'I'd put him in his early thirties. Probably a young executive. He'll be smartly dressed and arrive in a flashy car.'

On Tuesday at eight, the door-bell rang. On the door step stood a young man whose body seemed curiously wasted. His dough-grey face bore marks of suffering, his light brown hair was wispy, thinning on top and his shoulders drooped as though he had trouble bearing his own weight. He wore a stained, nylon, navy-blue track suit, red and white canvas shoes fraying at the toes and he wrung his hands nervously.

'I phoned last evening,' he said.

I watched my 'young executive' negotiate the two steps leading to our front door. His legs looked stiff. As he accompanied me to the lounge, I noticed he was not walking but hobbling. Alistair was a cripple.

He looked embarrassed as he perched uncomfortably on the edge of the settee. As I offered him coffee, he enquired apologetically, 'D'you mind if I smoke? I know it leaves a nasty smell in the house, but it takes the edge off the pain.'

'Are you in pain all the time?' I asked, glancing at his legs.

'Most of the time – especially on these damp winter days. I try to forget the pain, but it's not easy when you know what it's like to be healthy.'

'When did the pain start?'

My question was an open sesame. He forgot about *The Exorcist*. He told me that he used to have a very good job working on an oil rig in the North Sea.

'I loved that,' he recalled, 'the sea, the seasons, the wide open spaces. One day I had an accident. I fell – about forty feet, I think. I didn't break any bones but I was taken to a hospital where they gave me a tetanus injection. A precaution. There was a million to one chance of it happening, but the injection caused a side effect – something called serum sickness, a form of arthritis in the joints. I was paralysed from the waist down – my hips, knees, ankles and right wrist. I spent two years in hospital, another convalescing and then became a regular visitor to the outpatients departments at several hospitals. There was physiotherapy, manipulations under anaesthetic and numerous pills to ease the pain. Arthritis is a problem because it destroys the joints but the main problem's the pain. It's all right during the day but sometimes in the evening my joints become so stiff I have to use sticks. Or I shuffle around my flat on my bottom. Fortunately, I live on my own, so there's no one to see me when this happens. All hope of returning to my job has gone. My life-style's completely changed.'

'Have you many friends in Nottingham?' I asked.

'I used to – and I had a lot of money. I saved quite a lot when I was working. I've got a lovely flat. I used to drive expensive cars. Now I use alcohol as an anaesthetic. The money's dwindled and so have the friends. I can just about clamber on to a bike, but my knees won't bent sufficiently to pedal. The doctors say that in five years I must expect the joints to seize up completely.'

Alistair looked hopeless. Later, as I watched him disappear into the night, I felt hopeless too. I hoped he would come back to see us again.

The following Sunday evening he appeared at church. He was to come regularly, slipping into the service shyly and vanishing before the blessing was pronounced. He became a frequent visitor to our home. Sometimes he would be sober and we would talk about God. Sometimes he would be delivered by taxi, drunk. Alcohol was more than an anaesthetic; it was an addiction. Once he brought me a gift – an ash tray: 'To save you using your best saucers.'

For a year we prayed and waited and talked, but Alistair was unable or unwilling to respond to the love of God.

He was not the only one who was struggling. I was in conflict too. I would pray for Alistair regularly and on many occasions God would seem to underline passages from the Bible which reminded me of his power to heal. Even so, I wasn't sure that my faith would stretch that far. I had never witnessed a miracle and when people claimed that they had been miraculously healed, I had difficulty in believing.

But Alistair was deteriorating. He could never settle comfortably in a chair but would balance on the edge, shuffling and fidgeting to try to shift the pain. I would watch him wince and notice how he would swallow veganin straight from the tube as a child eats smarties. In between cigarettes he would tear paper handkerchiefs to shreds, ventilating his frustration as pain shot through his body.

One morning a letter arrived which jolted me into action. Jean Darnall was coming to speak at a meeting in the church hall underneath the rectory where we lived. I had heard of Jean Darnall and the way God had used her to minister healing. Was this God's answer for Alistair? I would talk to him about her and if he was willing to meet her, I would take this as a sign from God. He seemed interested, even excited. A meeting was arranged for Monday morning at ten.

The night before, Alistair was in church as usual, crouching in the corner of one of the side pews, as near invisible as possible. The church was full for the Guest Service.

'I can't remember the sermon, I'm afraid,' Alistair recalls, 'but I do remember that the preacher had a prayer at the end for those who didn't know the Lord and wanted to find him. During that prayer I forgot about my shyness, I forgot everyone. I found myself repeating the words of that prayer. They seemed to have been put into my lips by God himself.'

That night the search was over. A spiritual healing had taken place. When Alistair told me his face was alight with joy.

On Monday the world was bathed in sunshine. Nature seemed to be reminding us that winter was almost over, that spring was round the next corner. When I opened the door to Alistair, his face burst into an impish grin. He was fifteen minutes early.

'Would you like some coffee?' I asked.

'No, thanks. I'm too on edge to drink anything.'

He took out a cigarette, turned it over in his fingers, then thrust it back into his pocket. 'It doesn't seem quite the thing to do this morning – smoking I mean.'

The minutes ticked past so slowly that we both became tense.

Alistair played with the leaves trailing from the giant spider plant on the table beside him. I watched him, wondering how he was feeling, wondering how the Lord would honour our faith. When the door bell rang, we both jumped.

We heard my husband welcome Jean Darnall. The sound of her warm American accent floated in from the hall. I should have remembered to tell Alistair that Jean was not English.

Jean was relaxed as we concertined the events of Alistair's past seven years into a few sentences. She seemed deeply moved, especially by his faith. She asked one or two questions to locate the pain before explaining that she would simply lay her hands on Alistair and ask God to restore mobility to his limbs.

'Jean!' I stopped her. 'There's something I should tell you before you pray for Alistair. When you were living at Post Green, David and I lived in Poole. David was a curate. I was very critical of your ministry in those days, even cynical, and I want you to know I'm sorry.'

When Jean had listened to my confession and forgiven me we moved to the long settee, one on each side of Alistair. I sat and prayed silently. Jean stood beside him, laid her hands on his head and prayed quietly for his healing. The prayer was short, authoritative, unemotional.

I listened aghast as she then invited Alistair to thank God for his healing. He had been a Christian for only fourteen hours. He had never prayed aloud in his life.

His prayer was beautiful in its simplicity and child-like faith, as though he were conscious only of the Lord standing beside him.

Jean then told Alistair to kneel. I knew he couldn't. I had seen him sprawl at the communion rail. His knees were fixed, unable to bend. My eyes were rivetted as he first walked round the lounge, trying out his legs like a person testing a new pair of shoes. His face was radiant. Something wonderful was happening.

With a look of confidence which I had never seen before, he came striding towards the settee where we were sitting. He stood in front of us and looked me in the eye. I held my breath as the once-stiff joints flexed. He knelt. For several minutes he allowed his knees to hold his weight. 'I can't believe it,' he said, grinning from ear to ear. 'These knees haven't been able to bend for years.'

With a 'Praise the Lord!' Jean left to speak at her meeting. A little later I watched Alistair rush across the six-lane carriageway outside the rectory as strength surged through his limbs.

That lunch time, he made his way to Woolworths to buy an evening paper. As usual, the newspaper man sat on an upturned crate outside the store. As usual, he called out, 'Evening Post! Evening Post!' And, as usual, he looked up as Alistair approached him. But the cry, 'Evening Post' died on his lips as he watched Alistair, not hobbling across the pedestrian precinct, but walking with a spring in his step.

'What's happened?' he yelled.

Alistair grinned. He was no longer an arthritic. He could walk. He could run.

The euphoria lasted for days. Alistair threw away his pain killers, failed to keep a doctor's appointment and telephoned the outpatients' department to say he needed no further treatment. He later regretted these actions because it soon became apparent that vitality had returned to each damaged joint and weakened limb with one exception. Movement in his right foot sometimes continued to send sharp stabs of pain through his body; using the toes on that foot could cause pain.

We were perplexed but not daunted. God had wrought one miracle. Maybe this was to be a two-stage healing like the blind man who first saw men like trees walking and then received his sight fully.

We prayed for Alistair and laid hands on him, fully

expecting another miracle. We were so confident that this had happened that, after the prayer, I asked him to try walking along the cobbled pavement not far from the rectory. He returned crestfallen. His right foot continued to trouble him.

Alistair joined a cycling club where he made new friends and that summer would often cycle fifty miles into the countryside. As his legs, now strong, propelled the bicycle along country lanes to the wide open spaces, he gave silent thanks for his healing.

'Lord, what do you want us to do about his right foot?' I asked one day. As though in reply we were introduced to the ministry of 'soaking prayer', holding a specific need in the healing presence of God regularly. Praying for Alistair's foot became like cleaning my teeth in the morning.

One wet January day, Alistair was visiting Hartland Point in Devon with some friends. Although the wind was howling and the sea wild, they walked round the headland to explore a cave. Waves were thundering round the Point, crashing against the rocks. Suddenly they realised the tide was coming in fast. The angry sea was invading the beach. The pebbly shore was already awash, leaving only a narrow cobbled track for them to struggle along. The rocks and boulders were slippery and dangerous and Alistair was wearing canvas shoes. His right foot was hurting badly with the strain of the movement and the unevenness of the ground.

Suddenly, he found himself running without any pain in his right foot, as though the Lord was there, helping him across the granite boulders.

'I remember the waves threatening us with a watery grave,' he says, 'when suddenly everything went quiet. The noise of the sea disappeared. The cold and rain had gone. For a second I was no longer part of the danger; I was in the presence of God.'

That day his right foot was completely healed.

'I'd like to *do* something for God,' Alistair said after this second miracle. 'But the only thing I'm good at is cycling. So I'll cycle for God.'

The cycling club had announced an annual national event, the Twelve Hour Trials. Alistair was excited. If he entered for this, he could cycle for twelve hours and invite his friends to sponsor him, donating the proceeds to Tear Fund.

'Everyone at the club laughed when I said I was going in for the Twelve Hour,' he recalls. 'None of the lads there had ever dared try.'

He managed the first seven hours in the rain quite easily and finished up doing 241 miles. Twelve hours on a bike is a long time. Still wearing the red and white cycling cap, Alistair stumbled home to a hero's welcome. There could be no denying the extent of his healing now. He suffered for four or five days after that, not from arthritis, he was just saddle-sore.

A few weeks later, at a parish weekend, my husband invited Alistair to speak. The congregation heard how the Lord had met him in the Guest Service and how he had become a Christian. They listened spell-bound as he told them about the accident and tears welled up in many eyes as he spoke of his healing and bent his once-stiff knees. Then, in front of everyone, he knelt.

The ancient touch

Barry Kissel

The Rev. Barry Kissel, a New Zealander, has an itinerant ministry based on St Andrew's Church, Chorleywood. He is the author of *Springtime in the Church*, but is best known for his evangelistic ministry.

I was reading a fascinating book recently about village life in England one hundred and fifty years ago. Flora Thompson, the authoress, makes the following observation: 'There was no cripple, or mental defective in the hamlet and, except for a few months when a poor woman was dying of cancer, no invalid. Though food was rough and teeth were neglected, indigestion was unknown, while nervous troubles, there as elsewhere, had yet to be invented.'

Today, the more we seek to understand ourselves, the more complex we discover our natures to be. On the one hand we are human machines, motivated by a computer of incredible complexity, on the other we are jellies of wobbling emotions and feelings. The problem is that so often, for various reasons, we overload – part of the machine cuts out, and in various ways it affects the stability and running of the whole.

The most common form of 'cut out' is caused simply by nervous exhaustion. From my study I watch many of our community leaving in the morning for the city. At half past seven they stride down the hill, to reappear again twelve hours later with the same briefcases, which this time look even heavier. During the day the pressure has been enormous and in the evening there is the family, unfinished work from the office, and local commitments. Hanging over them, like a giant canopy, are the financial worries of living in suburbia today, mingled with fears of redundancy.

With a husband so involved in his work, the wife usually has the full responsibility of the children, plus running the home and organising the social life. From my base in suburbia I notice that mental and physical fatigue is one of the main causes for computer cut-out. Suddenly the mind is assailed by disjointed and disconnected thoughts. At times there are hallucinations, and the appearance and re-appearance of distorted faces and figures. Sleep becomes more and more difficult, and often there are severe physical manifestations.

In some instances what is needed is a withdrawal into the healing power of God's creation. The Psalmist observes, 'The heavens declare the glory of God and the vault of heaven proclaims his handiwork' (Psalm 19.1). And again Paul writes, 'Ever since God created the world, his everlasting power and deity, however invisible, have been there for the mind to see in the things he has made' (Romans 1.20).

Yet we are so conditioned to activity that even in the process of withdrawing into silence we feel as if we must somehow do something. At least we should pray or read scripture, or praise God in everything. Our concept of God is such that we cannot believe that he will take the initiative and do something first. This is folly, for we find that if we struggle to do something for God, then we just add to the clamour in our minds.

God's restoring power can be discovered in 'the being still and knowing' (Psalm 46.10). In the stillness of creation we absorb something of the orderliness and harmony of God – the rolling hills, the beautiful green of early summer, the buzzing insects, the granite rocks, the fauna of the forest floors, all speak peace and healing to our souls if we but stop and listen.

However, there are areas of the mind which don't go away by being still in the creation. These are the areas which have been hurt by bad experiences in the past.

We reap what we sow, but it is also true that we reap what others sow. This has become disturbingly obvious at the various universities and colleges with which I have been involved. The early sixties ushered in what has come to be called 'The Permissive Society'. At that time illegitimate children were conceived and marriages began to break up. In many cases these babies and children are now final year students at our places of education.

After a meeting in a large Victorian college chapel, we had a time for prayer with the laying on of hands. As I moved down the first row of twenty young people, I realised from conversation that every student had a deep emotional problem relating to traumas in childhood.

The mind is indeed like a computer and registers our experiences of life. It records the rejections, abuses, and hurts of those early years and now causes us to behave irrationally in certain areas of our personalities. A girl from an extremely wealthy home was overwhelmed with feelings of rejection. It transpired that her mother hadn't wanted her and during her pregnancy had had a nursery built on to the home, so that when the baby came it was put immediately into the hands of a nanny. She could never remember a time when either her father or mother had ever shown her any affection.

Healing begins when we seek Jesus. Experience shows that it is often helpful to have others pray with us. In the West Country I was staying at an old stone farmhouse which had a cellar which had not been opened in living memory. Being rather curious, I went to inspect it and found that the door was bolted and locked by an enormous old-fashioned padlock, the key of which had long since been lost. I imagined that behind the door there was a collection of household items that had been put away to be mended, or attended to, at another time. Alas, fear and superstition may result in the door staying locked for another hundred years.

When the Holy Spirit comes, he initially breaks the padlock, pulls back the iron bars, and allows the hidden, unresolved hurts to emerge into the daylight. This can be a disturbing experience as often the fear, although it has been locked away in the cellar, has somehow permeated the whole house. It is into this situation that the Holy Spirit comes, like oil, seeping into every cavity and nook.

For a person who has been deeply hurt, this process can continue at various intervals over a period of many years. This is why community of committed people is helpful for support and encouragement.

Because of traumatic experiences in the past, our minds react in certain preconditioned ways in the present. We had a door in our home which, because of the damp weather, had warped and only ever opened half way. My mind was so conditioned that even after I had shaved a piece off the base, for a period of time I still only opened it half way. I was free to act differently but my mind needed, through a conscious act of my will, to be re-programmed.

When seeking God's healing, problems may be caused by the tendency to slip back into old reactions after the obvious initial freedom. At such times we are tempted to think that maybe nothing happened to us after all, and that the supposed healing was an illusion.

At this time we need to draw upon the Word and the Sacrament. The word of God is 'like a lamp to our feet and a light to our path' (Psalm 119.105), and the promises of God are to be trusted. It is often helpful to copy out a Scripture such as Philippians 4.8: 'Fill your minds with everything that is true, everything that is noble, everything that is good and pure, everything that we love and honour, and everything that can be thought virtuous or worthy of praise; then the peace of God will be with you.'

In writing about the Lord's Supper (1 Corinthians 2.30–31), Paul suggests that the wrong use of this Sacrament can lead to weakness, illness, and even death. How much more, then, will the right use lead to wholeness of life. We always encourage people to seek the continuing healing of Christ every time they take the Sacrament. A man was telling me recently that he had had an unresolved wrong attitude towards his mother which went back as long as he could remember. Because of this he was experiencing the beginnings of a stomach ulcer. He asked Christ to break into the situation and testified that the ultimate healing came over a period of time through the Sacrament.

Before we move away from the mind, it is important to realise that this is the battlefield upon which the devil wages his war. He is by nature a destroyer, a liar, and an accuser. It is to the mind that he brings the thoughts which, if pursued, can lead to oppression. It is not without significance that Paul writes: 'Always carry the shield of faith so that you can use it to put out the burning arrows of the Evil One' (Ephesians 6.16).

'Burning arrows', once they pierce, and make an entrance, consume and destroy. On the walls of Luther's study there is a mark where he threw the inkpot at the devil. We at times need to be just as definite. We must heed the words of Peter when he wrote: 'Be calm, but vigilant, because your enemy, the Devil, is prowling round like a roaring lion looking for someone to eat. Stand up to him, strong in faith' (1 Peter 5.8–9).

Whether we call it 'possession' or 'oppression', it is my experience that the powers of evil are able somehow to infiltrate the human personality and distort it. In the final service at the end of a week's mission, a young Christian came seeking freedom. He wanted to be engaged to a certain girl, but was also a practising homosexual. He had tried to free himself but always, in his words, something overwhelmed him. As I prayed for him in the name of Jesus, he shook violently and began to say, 'I'm free, I'm free – something has left me.' In his particular case, something had.

At a meeting for neighbours in a home, a young wife

committed her life to Christ, and when I enquired about her husband, she told me a strange story. They had been married three years and had just had a baby. During the whole of that time there were only three places her husband would go to – his parents' home, his work, and his own home. In any other situation he was just enveloped in a tremendous fear and had to leave. It was as if something overcame him. The following night I prayed for him and led him to Christ. He was so wonderfully delivered that the following Sunday morning they both attended a place of worship.

In *The Living Bible* there is a delightful translation of Jude, verse 21. It reads: 'Stay always within the boundaries where God's love can reach and bless you.' When we step outside the boundaries through wilful disobedience or ignorance, we can suffer from destructive feelings of guilt and insecurity, and these can also have physical effects.

A Christian lady came to me in much distress. Seven years previously she had stepped outside the boundaries and had an affair. At the same time she had contracted a crippling internal disease which left her weak and in need of constant medical care. Before I met her she had come to a deep sense of sorrow and, through confession, had sought the forgiveness of Christ.

I had been speaking on the truth that God 'forgives us our sins and cleanses us from all unrighteousness' (1 John 1.9). She had known God's forgiveness, but felt that her physical condition was due to her wrong actions and that what she needed was God's cleansing. As we prayed for cleansing, the physical condition was resolved.

In this healing ministry, it would seem that many of the gifts of the Spirit are in operation (1 Corinthians 12.4–11). The 'word of knowledge' is one. Obviously God knows everything about every person, and the 'word of knowledge' is a divinely given fragment of that knowledge. We were at Waltham Abbey and a young married couple came for prayer. The husband told us that his wife was often overwhelmed by the fear of death and that this caused a great deal of sadness in her life. As he said this, the Holy Spirit told me that it was all related to her mother. On conveying that to her she broke down and wept. She told me that her mother had died when she was four and we were able to minister the deliverance and healing of Christ at this point.

Another gift is that of 'faith'. We had John Wimber and a team of thirty of his church from California visit us in Chorleywood. They are part of a remarkable work of God. Beginning with a group of forty members four years ago, they now number three and a half thousand. Their evangelistic ministry is one of healing through the operation of the Spirit's gifts of the 'word of knowledge' and 'faith'.

I was praying with a group of them for a lady who was a relative of a member of our congregation. She had completely lost the sight in her left eye and was seeking healing. A number of us stood around her as we waited for a revelation from the Lord. Although I believe in physical healing through prayer, I did not at that moment have faith to believe that her eye would be healed. However, a young man in the group did. He laid his hands on her and quietly told her that Jesus was at that moment restoring her sight. As a bystander I was as surprised as everyone else proved to be when, with delight, she claimed to have restored sight. For the last year that has certainly been the case. At the moment of prayer the Lord had given the young man the gift of faith.

Vividly I remember one of the occasions when I felt in possession of an incredible certainty which was this gift of faith. A young man who had slight connections with our church was involved in a late night head-on crash. His car was written off and when eventually the ambulance arrived, he was pulled out as if dead. At the hospital I visited the Intensive Care Unit and spoke with the medical team

136

involved. They said that his life was only being maintained by a machine and that his prognosis was non-existent. I accepted their diagnosis and made my way towards his cubicle to pray with him. As I entered the area I was given an inner certainty that the Lord was going to raise him to life. When I came to pray I found myself praising God for the healing which was beginning. Suffice it to say, he eventually recovered.

Paul uses the term 'the gifts of healing' in 1 Corinthians 12.4–11. There are various ways in which the Lord shows Christians what particular healing gift they may have. For fourteen years we have prayed regularly for the sick at our monthly evening Communion Service. Five or six church leaders usually minister and they pray in such a way that the whole church can join in. This changed with the coming of John Wimber. On the Saturday night of his visit he had a word of knowledge to the effect that the Lord was anointing different members of the congregation for a healing ministry. He went on to say that all those who felt a warm tingling in their hands should go to the communion rail. About thirty went forward. He then anointed them with oil in the name of the Lord and the Spirit came mightily upon them.

Looking back over twelve months, the reality of this is still there, and after every service a team of these folk is on hand to pray for the sick. It is amongst them that we feel a gift of healing. To illustrate – one morning a lady came forward in great emotional distress. As I prayed I sensed the Lord say two things: firstly, she was to open her life fully to him and to receive the resources of his Spirit; secondly, she was to make an appointment to see a member of our congregation, who is a doctor and a trained counsellor.

The 'discerning of spirits' is the final gift I have experienced in this ministry. In the West Country a girl came for counsel. As I looked at her I was inwardly aware that evil had infiltrated her personality. She said that she had wanted to believe in Jesus, but whenever she tried, voices screamed in her head and she became agitated and violent. It transpired that she had been actively involved in occult practices. As she repented a prayer in the name of Jesus set her free to believe and rejoice.

I believe that, apart from unbelief, the greatest barrier to healing is an unwillingness to be healed. It may sound strange, but many people only have identity and receive the compassion they desire because of their illness.

One evening the theme of my talk had been on Jesus' question, 'Do you want to be healed?' A young engaged couple stayed behind to talk. The girl suffered from noises in the inner ear, which sometimes became so severe that she fainted. Over the years her parents had taken her to many doctors, but extensive tests showed nothing organically wrong.

Her conversation turned into a confession. When she was young her father had not been able to show her affection. However, at an early age she discovered that if she fainted she would receive the affection she craved. With the fainting came the noises in the inner ear. She had received both medical care and Christian prayer, and she had enjoyed the attention; up until that day she hadn't wanted to be healed. Her subsequent letter recounts that after her prayer of confession, the Lord healed her completely.

As I conclude this statement of my conviction and experience of healing, I am surrounded by imponderables – by sick children that we have regularly prayed for, anointed with oil, fasted for, spent nights corporately in prayer for, and who are still sick, to say nothing of the dear friends who are still desperately depressed after hours of counselling and loving care and concern, or of others who have suffered the agony of cancer. I am not a 'triumphalist' and do not believe that God heals everyone in this life.

I am an evangelist. Over the years I have seen hundreds of people make commitments to Jesus Christ in response to gospel messages. Recently I was reading in an old diary about a group of forty people who had professed conversion one summer. Of that group, I know of only ten who are still involved in Christian worship and witness. I don't understand that, but I have an inner conviction that the gospel is true and there are enough genuinely changed lives to warrant this conviction. It is on the same basis that I pray for the sick with a commission and command of Jesus that has never been withdrawn.

The pathway to healing

Eric Britt

The Rev. Eric Britt is an Anglican vicar in Essex. He writes of his own agonising and perplexing illness and of his remarkable deliverance.

It all began some eleven years ago, five months after I had married Sue. At the time of our wedding neither of us realised how early on in our married life those words 'in sickness and in health' were going to have to be worked out in our day to day living.

I was at the time a student at St John's Theological College, Nottingham, training for the ordained ministry. It was the Christmas vacation and we were planning to go home to Aldershot for the Christmas celebrations. The day began as any other day, and I busied myself getting things organised, so that when my wife returned from work we would be ready to set off on the four hour journey. I decided to have a bath – nothing unusual in that – except from that point on began a seven year struggle with physical, emotional and spiritual pain. As I tried to get out of the bath, I doubled up in pain. I felt as if a sword had gone into my right side. At first I thought it was a severe 'stitch', but the pain increased, and I could hardly move. I eventually managed to crawl round to our next door neighbours, with a towel wrapped around me, and there I collapsed. The doctor was called and came fairly quickly. He prescribed pain killers, assuring me that it would be quite safe to drive to Aldershot, and that it was 'just one of those unexplainable things.'

For many years I was to live with 'those unexplainable things' which resulted in a painful pilgrimage, and on occasions a very lonely one. Eventually I was subjected to various kidney investigations, along with an IVP X-ray, but the doctors seemed to be reluctant to state categorically what was wrong. I was ready for them to tell me that it was psychosomatic (I knew from my studies what the mind could do to the body), but I was assured that this was not the case. Early on I was prescribed 'pethidine' to be taken when required, and it became increasingly necessary. The trouble was I started to become addicted, but fortunately I realised, and one afternoon ceremonially flushed them down the toilet. I was becoming more and more dissatisfied with my treatment and arranged to change from my local doctor to the health clinic at Nottingham University, only to undergo once again all the tests relating to kidney problems. By this time, I seemed to be living on pain-killing tablets, and twice collapsed at College and was taken to hospital and the health clinic. Renal colic was what the doctors said I had, but they could not explain why it kept recurring.

Some eighteen months passed, and I had lost a stone and a half. I was admitted to St Luke's Clinic for the Clergy in London to undergo two weeks of intensive tests with a Harley Street specialist. At last there seemed to be a glimmer of hope as the IVP X-ray taken at University College Hospital showed that one of the tubes in my right kidney was kinked. Discussion about what to do ranged over the whole spectrum, including the possibility of removing the right kidney. However, there was concern that the left kidney might not be able to cope, and in any event, it did not account for the constant pain. The kidney was slightly faulty, but this did not justify its removal at this stage.

Eventually one of the tests showed a high calcium content in my blood – at last something positive. I was immediately put upon a drug called Allopurinol, and things seemed to improve. I was told that I would probably be on this drug for the rest of my life, which didn't

143

seem too much of a hardship, especially if it got rid of this constant pain.

So at last, I thought, I could go forward into the future without this dark cloud overshadowing me – but it was not to be.

Some two and a half years had by now elapsed, and during that time I had constantly asked the question, 'Why, God?' It was during these years, also, that I began to allow God into the recesses of my mind, for if my pain was in some way related to inner turmoil (present or past) I wanted God to deal with it. Through the ministry of Mrs Marjorie Dalton, a Christian lady whom God had used greatly in healing, I began to experience healing of the memories. The Holy Spirit brought to light many events from the past, the consequences of which I was still living with, even if deeply submerged in my sub-conscious. There, in the lounge of Marjorie's house, I was to come face to face with suppressed hatred and unforgiveness, bitterness and insecurity, and for two hours one afternoon I sobbed my heart out, as the knots inside began to unwind.

There was a change – people noticed and commented upon it, but it was not the answer to my physical pain. I still could not go out into the town or country without taking a supply of pain killing tablets with me for I never knew when I might double up in pain. My right hand seemed to be constantly resting upon my right side in an effort to ease the discomfort.

I felt a total failure. I could do very little around the house; after about twenty minutes of decorating a room or digging the garden, I would have to stop because of the pain in my side. I felt it was all so unfair – especially to Sue. What sort of husband was I being to her? As if this wasn't enough, I also felt a failure as a student. I struggled with my studies and the discipline of a theological college. Having to attend chapel daily became an ordeal: I was there in body, but not in spirit. I felt desperately alone and one day I broke down. Two of my closest friends were nearby and they took me home. For two weeks I couldn't face anyone. I would go out in the car perhaps to a country church and just sit. Yet, in a strange way, in the midst of this isolation, I felt God was there, and there was an inner conviction that I would eventually come out of this dark tunnel. With the prayers and help of friends I did. I learnt to live with the niggling pain, the daily drug taking, and so life continued.

My time at college came to an end, and Sue and I moved to our new parish of Chorleywood in Hertfordshire. A fresh chapter was about to begin; the drugs I was on seemed to have got things sorted out, and I was feeling stronger in body, mind and spirit. For the first year of my curacy I was fine. Sue was expecting our first child, and I was incredibly happy. Then came an eventful visit to my local doctor, who was still taking a regular blood sample from me. He expressed concern over the long term effect of the drug Allopurinol and felt it was possible that I could come off them, and so I did. One week later I was once more doubled up in pain. More blood tests followed and I was back on Allopurinol, but this time it didn't seem to make any difference. In that short period of being off the drug I had created more grit which was once more lodged in the right kidney. And so the whole process began again with IVP X-rays, visits to yet more specialists, and never any positive suggestions, only the totally useless comment, 'You'll have to live with it.' I was angry with the doctors, I was angry with myself and I was very angry with God. At one stage in the bathroom cabinet there were six different bottles of tablets, pain-killing and anti-depressant.

Then there came another ray of hope – my local doctor, who was a Christian, himself determined to get to the bottom of this problem. Early on in my records was the account of my midnight dash across London in an ambulance, when I was living in Putney. The medical records showed suspected appendicitis – 'Was your appendix taken out?' the doctor asked.

'No,' was my reply. 'I was kept in hospital for a week, and told it was a stone in the kidney.'

Had they been right? Was it really my kidney that was creating all the problem? Was it really the high calcium in my blood? Could the answer be the removal of my appendix? A trip to Harley Street the following week confirmed that the appendix was in a state – that was on a Thursday, and the following Sunday I was in the Middlesex Hospital waiting for an operation to remove my appendix. I recovered remarkably quickly and ten days later was sunning myself in Spain. I tried to convince myself that everything was now all right, but the reality of the situation was that I still had the niggling pain. In the end I resorted to taking the pain killing tablets again, but somehow I was afraid to tell anyone. Eventually I had to admit that I was still in pain – twice more I doubled up in pain – once as I raised my hands to give the blessing in church. That was unusual, for by now I could tell when something like this was going to happen, and could quickly arrange for a pain-relieving injection.

In the midst of this, I was having to continue to minister. People came to be counselled, an increasing number began to seek the laying-on of hands, and they did seem to benefit. I continued all the outward signs of ministry, but inside I had stopped ministering. What was the point? I was fed up with trying to count the number of times I had received the laying-on of hands – what difference had it made to me? I was still ill. I would do it for others, because it was part of my job, but inwardly I felt it was a waste of time.

I fought against the inner turmoils, but there were times when I became very depressed. It wasn't just a matter of physical pain, it was all that went with it – especially the recurring sense of failure – and what of the future?

The crisis came in March 1977. Walking in Rickmansworth High Street, I once more doubled up in pain. I struggled back to the car and cried. I could go on no longer and decided that something had to be done. I had by now seen several different specialists, but the present one happened to be a Christian. I knew that he held a clinic every Wednesday morning at Watford Hospital. So I determined to go, and insisted on seeing him. I arrived early Wednesday morning and saw the receptionist nurse, who by this time knew me well. I pleaded with her to let me see the doctor, even though I didn't have an appointment. Ten minutes later I was with the specialist, and for half-an-hour I unburdened myself – the failure, the anger, the frustration all came flowing forth. At the end the doctor prayed with me and then suggested he injected into one of the muscles in my back. I didn't know what it was, but was later to discover it was simply a local anesthetic to kill the pain.

The following Sunday evening we were to have a visit from Jean Darnell to preach and conduct a healing service. Many of my friends hoped I would go forward for her ministry, but unknown to them I had determined not to be disappointed yet again. That evening was very eventful: the atmosphere was charged as we saw the evidence of Christ's healing power in our midst. Jean discerned certain conditions and illnesses in folk as they came forward for prayer. The staff took it in turn to pray with Jean, and whilst I was sitting down, having taken my part, I prayed, 'Lord, if you want me to go forward for prayer, you'll have to tell Jean exactly what is wrong with me.' It never happened! Well, not in the service. After the two and a half hour service, we all went into the church lounge for coffee and biscuits – there had been a lot to take in. I chatted a little while, and then went to Jean who was standing in the middle of the room, to say goodbye. I duly said the right things, and was turning to go home, when Jean put her hand on my shoulder and said, 'Eric, I want to pray with you.'

'Here!' I replied.

'Yes, do you mind?'

What could I say? 'No – it's OK.'

I looked around the room. Everyone seemed to be smiling as if to say, 'See Eric you can't get away.'

What was to follow, was something I will never forget – standing there in the middle of the room Jean prayed in tongues as she laid her hands on my shoulders. Then she spoke in English, and it was as if she had my medical file in front of her. She had been so busy all day that I knew no one could have briefed her, and in any case very few knew all the details. But she then spoke some words, which were to go deep into my heart. I believe they were words from God as she spoke, 'Eric as you minister so shall you be strengthened.' How did she know that I had stopped ministering? How did she knew how weak I was feeling?

I left Jean perplexed and yet thrilled. Outwardly there was no difference, yet inwardly I knew something had happened. I said nothing. I continued to go for my blood tests and various other tests, including the annual IVP X-ray. But I was no longer in pain. I came off the Allopurinol, and started to go out without taking pain-killing tablets with me. I was able to walk without that constant niggling and I could dig the garden without having to give up after twenty minutes. Sue noticed the difference, and so did others but I said nothing. I wanted to be sure this time that it would last.

We moved to Frimley that following October, and dutifully I went to see my new doctor. My file had not come through, so I explained why I was there – I had a quarterly blood test. He wanted to know why and so I gave him my potted medical history. He looked perplexed, 'You are sure it was Allopurinol you were on?'

'Yes,' I replied!

'But if you are on that drug, you're on it for life,' said the doctor.

'Well, I'm sorry but I used to be on it, but no longer.'

He quickly took a blood sample, and a week later interrogated me further, and took another blood sample – all the results were perfectly all right. He sent a tracer for my records and on my next visit said, 'I just don't understand.' I still said nothing. I waited and felt I had to wait two years before speaking of my experience that night with Jean Darnell.

We only stayed in Frimley two and a half years, and before leaving, I went once again to see the Christian doctor in Watford hospital. I asked him whether the injection I had received just prior to Jean's visit could explain why my blood was now normal, and why I was now no longer creating excessive grit. He assured me that the injection had been simply to kill the pain and nothing else. There was no medical explanation for my improvement. At last I felt free to testify to my healing, which I do today – some five years from the date of that healing service. You might ask, 'But why was the healing delayed?' I am not sure that I can give a satisfactory answer. The years of illness were an agonising and perplexing period in my life, yet through it I believe God has helped me to empathise with those who go through similar experiences, and have to live with uncertainty, pain, failure, and anger. I believe God is continuing his healing work within me. Although I am still left with questions, I now pray for others, knowing that whilst it might be years before they are whole, in body, mind and spirit, no prayer is unheard by God. The pilgrimage they may have to walk will, if handed over to him, bring light to others.

The power of the cross

John Gunstone

The Rev. John Gunstone is the County Ecumenical Officer for Greater Manchester and was formerly chaplain at Whatcombe House, Dorset. He is the author of several books published by Hodder and Stoughton and the S.P.C.K. His latest one is *Pentecostal Anglicans*.

I was certain we were about to witness a miracle.

A man who had been blind since early childhood had come to a conference on healing at Whatcombe House. He was convinced God was going to restore his sight. He talked openly about his conviction; he said he knew the weekend would be one of healing for him.

His simple faith and sense of expectancy impressed the community. We discussed his case among ourselves and prayed earnestly for him. How wonderful if his sight *was* restored at a conference on healing!

On the Sunday afternoon I presided at the final Eucharist in the large, bright lounge of the house, crowded with guests and members of the community. As usual, after we had received the Sacrament, I invited those present to make requests for prayer.

It was then that the blind man asked us to pray for his healing.

I felt a mixture of excitement and apprehension bubble up inside me as I stepped over to where he was kneeling. His hands were held up in supplication; his sightless eyes glistened.

'Praise you, Lord!' he muttered. 'Thank you, Jesus!'

Beads of sweat dribbled down his forehead as my hands closed over him. I could feel his whole body trembling.

I forced myself to forget him and the other people in the room. I tried to relax and listen to the Lord.

After praying quietly in tongues for a while, I spoke aloud. I asked our heavenly Father that Jesus might be glorified by the restoration of his servant's sight. I crushed a sudden impulse to add the words, 'If it be your will.'

There was a long pause. The silence in the room was stiffling. Slowly I took my hands away from his head, my heart pounding, my mouth dry.

Nothing happened.

A murmur of prayer rose from the others. Everyone was concentrating with eyes shut. Some were standing, others were sitting or kneeling.

Lord, may he receive his sight! . . . *Please*, Lord!

Still nothing happened.

Slowly I returned to my chair. The atmosphere in the room subsided as the people stopped praying, looked round, and resumed their seats.

The final hymn, the last prayer, and the Eucharist was over.

We drifted into the hall for tea. The guests were talking in a restrained fashion among themselves. No one mentioned the incident, but I could sense their disappointment.

The blind man, led by his wife, approached me. I braced myself as I took his hand.

'Thank you for praying!' he said, squeezing me in his powerful grip.

His eyes were still shining, and he smiled at me.

I said something inconsequential, and then he was gone . . .

That was ten years ago, but every detail is as clear to me now as if it had happened only yesterday.

At the time of my ordination, I suppose I had what was a fairly typical attitude among Anglican clergy towards the ministry of healing. As a curate in West Ham and as a vicar in Romford, I visited the sick members of the congregation at home or in hospital, chatting with them for a while and saying a collect and the Lord's Prayer with them before I left. If they were ill for any length of time, I took them communion from the reserved sacrament and added their names to the intercession list that was read out at services on Sundays.

I was not aware that the prayers or the sacrament had any dynamic effect on them. Some said they'd 'been helped' by the prayers and 'felt better' after receiving communion. My basic assumption was that this ministry offered them a means of support rather than a gift of healing.

That assumption was challenged after I had a Pentecostal experience of baptism in the Holy Spirit in 1963.

From that time, I began to meet Christians who believed that God answered prayers for healing directly and that such healings were a gift of the Spirit operating through the church. I also began to meet people who had experienced this kind of healing.

One evening I went along to a prayer group in my parish with a heavy cold. I should have stayed at home and gone to bed early, but I didn't like to miss this group, for it offered me a spiritual support I had rarely known before. The members of the group were suitably sympathetic. Then, while we were praying together, one of them got up and laid hands on me for healing. Next day every trace of the cold had gone.

A small thing, perhaps, but it had a profound influence on me. Colds generally hang around me for a week or more: this one disappeared overnight. But what was more important was that the one who had prayed was a lay person, and no lay person had ever laid hands on me before. Furthermore – and this was even more startling – that person was a woman!

Thus I was introduced to the ministry of healing through a spiritual gift to a member of my own congregation.

A year or two later another member of the congregation became chronically ill with a deteriorating disease in the upper part of her spine. Eileen (as I will call her) was in and out of hospital for weeks at a time. She was in constant pain; she had to wear a surgical collar.

The crisis came when her surgeon at the London Hospital said she ought to consider having an operation. This would, he said, halt the spread of the disease and relieve her pain, but he feared it would paralyse her from the waist downwards for the rest of her life.

It was then that I began to pray for her healing regularly with anointing and the laying-on of hands. Gradually this developed into a monthly church service of prayer for healing.

The service never attracted large numbers. I didn't advertise it, relying on news of it passing round by word of mouth. I invited those who came to bring a prayer partner with them, and I suppose the largest number we ever had was about twenty.

On the day of the service I spent more time than usual in prayer and kept a simple fast. The service itself was straightforward – no singing, no emotional exhortations. There was a Bible reading, a brief address, a few general prayers, and then those who wished came and knelt at the communion rail or sat in the front pew while I anointed them and laid hands on them.

During the first few occasions I used a printed form of prayer, but I soon abandoned that in favour of spontaneous praying. When I laid hands on each one, I tried to speak as the Spirit led me. Often what I said seemed especially appropriate for the person concerned – or so they told me afterwards.

There were some healings. A man with a severe migraine was cured and the pain never returned. A woman was delivered from a persistent fear which she had had since childhood.

And in some other cases people's conditions improved. A woman who was going blind recovered sufficiently to be able to see with the aid of special glasses. Another woman's fractured arm was healed in record time.

As far as Eileen was concerned, there was no obvious

healing, but the deterioration of her spine was checked sufficiently for the surgeon to postpone the dreaded operation. And she faced her ordeal with increasing faith. I owe her a great deal. Without her, I do not think I would have continued with the services.

When I left Romford in 1971 and joined the Barnabas Fellowship at Whatcombe House in Dorset, my involvement in the ministry of healing developed considerably. Among the two thousand or so people who stayed with the community each year, many came for healing, and I spent hours with other members of the fellowship ministering to them.

There were remarkable healings – much to praise the Lord for. And praise him we did! But my general impression is that it was people with emotional and spiritual problems who were helped the most. Only a few with serious physical illnesses were healed; some, like the blind man, were not healed at all.

It isn't easy to write like this. With the spread of the ministry of healing in the denominations in recent years, there has grown up a triumphalism in some quarters – a false triumphalism that regards any suggestion of failure as an indication of faithlessness and hardness of heart.

You must never say that God doesn't heal, it is argued. Didn't Jesus promise that 'whatever you ask in my name, I will do it, that the Father may be glorified in the Son' (John 14.13)? When you pray for healing, you must believe you receive that healing as a gift from him. Even if there is no immediate indication of it, you must claim it by faith and carry on as if the symptoms didn't exist.

In its extreme form, this false triumphalism discourages reliance on professional medical advice and skill.

Now I realise, that one of our weaknesses as Christians today is our lack of faith in God's healing power. Too often in the past we have assumed that suffering is a cross sent to us by God and that healing is solely the business of the medical profession. To counter that weakness, a vigorous reaffirmation of the New Testament teaching on the gift of healing and all it implies is necessary.

But this false triumphalism goes too far. To tell the sick that they are to believe they are healed when it is evident that they are not, is dishonouring to God. When Jesus Christ heals, he really does heal, and the fruit of his healing is wholeness – salvation – in mind and spirit as well as in body. There is certainly no place in it for self-deception.

If we are not healed in answer to prayer, the truthful thing to do is to admit it. It could be that there is a blockage somewhere, preventing God's grace from reaching us. Maybe it is a lack of faith on our part, or on the part of those ministering to us. Maybe our sinfulness is getting in the way, or our willingness to change, or our disregard of the doctor's advice.

But it could also be that we are caught up in the mystery of this world's suffering and death in such a way that healing is not possible in our case – or not possible yet. It is a fact of life that we are dying men and women – and none of us can escape the consequences of that.

Death came eventually to those whom Jesus healed and to those whom he raised from the dead – Jairus' daughter, the widow's son at Nain, and Lazarus. Suffering and death also came to Jesus himself.

In our enthusiasm to proclaim the kingdom of God through the healing gifts of the Spirit, we must not forget that it was through the passion and crucifixion of Christ himself that our salvation was won. Jesus prayed in Gethsemane that he might be delivered from such suffering. 'In the days of his flesh, Jesus offered up prayers and supplications, with loud cries and tears, to him who was able to save him from death, and he was heard for his godly fear' (Hebrews 5.7).

But how was he heard? Not by being protected from the cross, but by being strengthened to accept it for the sins of the world. The Father answered the Son's prayer by raising him victoriously over sin and death.

The New Testament does not solve the problem of suffering and death, but it provides us with a deep insight into what these terrible things can mean for us. Because Christians are already beginning to share in the risen life of Christ here and now through the Holy Spirit, the sufferings which we encounter and the death which ultimately faces us can be the means of greater union with God.

Jesus commanded his disciples, 'Heal the sick . . . and say, The kingdom of God has come here to you' (Luke 10.9). The ministry of healing continues that proclamation.

But the kingdom of God is revealed in other ways, too. When the disciples claimed a privileged place in that kingdom, Jesus asked them, 'Are you able to be baptised with the baptism with which I am baptised?' (Mark 10.29).

That insight gives the apostolic teaching in the New Testament a triumphant note: but it is triumph in the power of the cross, not in the power to heal.

The Church's healing ministry has to be set against this fuller perspective of the gospel. The way to Easter and Pentecost lies through Maundy Thursday and Good Friday. A false triumphalism about healing ignore this. To 'ask in Jesus' name' can involve much more than requests for healing.

Alongside the stories of wonderful healings, then, I want to put other stories of gifts of grace which came to me through those who were not healed physically. I have known people who drew so close to Jesus Christ in their sufferings that when I was with them I was humbled and awed at the presence of God.

Once when I was on holiday in Dublin I visited the relative of a friend who was desperately ill. As I went through the gates of the institution in which she was confined, I saw in big letters over the entrance, 'Hospital for the Incurables'. What a greeting for any patient being carried in on a stretcher!

The sick woman lay in bed paralysed with pain. She could hardly move a limb or her head. Every breath was a battle. Yet the drab green cubicle seemed flooded with light. Patience, faith, joy, thankfulness – they flowed from her like a strange power. Before I left, I prayed with her and pronounced a blessing over her, but I had no doubt that God's real blessing was coming from her to me.

She epitomised what Paul meant when he said, 'This slight momentary affliction is preparing us for an eternal weight of glory beyond all comparison, because we look not to the things that are seen but to the things that are unseen' (2 Corinthians 4.17–18).

About a year after I left Romford, Eileen visited Whatcombe and was counselled by a member of the community about her condition. My successor in the parish had continued the services of prayer for healing, and Eileen had still not had to have the operation, but her spine was no better.

When she got back home, she realised more clearly than before how bitter she had become about her troubles. At length she prayed, 'Lord, if I have to go through life with all this pain, please take away my bitterness.'

A few weeks later, when she was at the service, she felt a burning pain in her neck as the vicar laid hands on her. It continued for two or three days.

She was due to see the surgeon again the following week. What happened then she described on a cassette she sent me some weeks later: 'As the surgeon examined me, feeling each vertebra from the base of the spine upwards, I felt no pain, which was unusual. He seemed puzzled, and he sent me for an X-ray, marking the note, "Urgent".

'When the X-ray film came back, he looked at it for a long time, and then asked the orthopaedic surgeon to come and see it as well. The orthopaedic surgeon also examined my spine very thoroughly. He seemed puzzled, too.

159

'They asked me what I had been doing that week. Very nervously, I said that I hadn't been doing anything, except that my vicar had anointed me for healing a few days' previously. I told them how my neck had burned when he laid hands on me, and you could see the looks of surprise on their faces.

'Then they had a quiet chat together, and when that was finished, they invited me to look at the X-ray plates they had been examining. On one plate, which had been taken three weeks ago, I could see the fibrous tissues blurring the image of the spine, but on the other plate – the one that had just been taken – the vertebrae stood out quite clearly.

'"You can take your collar off," they said to me, "and we'll trust you'll never have to wear it again. This is nothing less than a miracle."'

Eileen left the hospital, slipped into a nearby church, and sobbed her thanksgiving to God. A blockage had been removed; a healing had been given. Her life since then has been one of encouragement and comfort to many sick people.

I rang her up just before I wrote this piece to ask for her permission to tell her story. There was a long pause on the other end of the line before she answered; then she said: 'Yes, but remember there's more to healing than the cure of physical symptoms. The Lord still has a lot of inner healing to do in me yet!'

Maybe our vision of God's healing work is always too narrow, too undiscerning.

Take that blind man, for example. Two or three years after the incident I have described, I met a friend of his who had been with him on that weekend, and I enquired about him.

'Oh, he's fine!' said the friend. 'Still praising the Lord!'

'Has he been healed, then?' I asked.

The friend shook his head.

'No . . . but he still believes his sight will be restored one day.'